On Assimilation: A Ranger's Return From War

By: Leo Jenkins

First published in Colorado Springs, CO in 2014 by Blackside Publishing: PO Box 63925 Colorado Springs, CO 80962

Email: publishing@blacksideconcepts.com

ISBN: 978-0991286577

Foreword by Marty Skovlund
Cover design by Jarred Taylor
Formatting and margins by Matthew Sanders

For a catalog of all books published by Blackside Publishing please contact:

Blackside Publishing: PO Box 63925 Colorado Springs, CO 80962

www.blacksidepublishing.com
www.tfblacktraining.com

Front cover image: © Jarred Taylor

Table of Contents

"I should not obtrude my affairs so much on the notice of my readers if very particular inquiries had not been made by my townsmen concerning my mode of life, which some would call impertinent, though they do not appear to me at all impertinent, but, considering the circumstances, very natural and pertinent.... I should not talk so much about myself if there were anybody else whom I knew as well. Unfortunately, I am confined to this theme by the narrowness of my experience....As for the rest of my readers, they will accept such portions as apply to them."

~Henry David Thoreau

Dedication

This book is dedicated to the tens of millions of veterans who have, at some point, felt alone in a crowded room. This is for those who have readily displayed the intestinal fortitude to stand up and say, "Here I am, send me!" when times got tough.

Additionally, had it not been for the loving support of my family and close friends I never would have survived long enough to author this book. Dad, Piper, Stacy, Ashley, Joel, Mike, Stacy, Mark, Jess, Anna, Matt, Nathan and so many others, thank you for always being there, keeping me afloat when I didn't have the strength to swim on my own.

Foreword

I remember sitting on my couch in central New York, still on active duty with the Army, discussing a possible separation from the military with my wife. We talked about where we would move if I 'got out', and what we would do for work. We both liked the idea of Colorado, so I began to do some research. My wife and I, both avid participants of CrossFit, were browsing the Facebook pages of some of the local gyms in Colorado Springs and brainstorming which ones we might want to join if we moved there.

Scrolling down through the pictures of a recent competition hosted at CrossFit SoCo, I came across a few shots of a bearded competitor who was obviously in good shape. He had tattoos, looked a little rough around the edges, and most noticeably – he was wearing a pink and white shirt that was at least two sizes two small with the word 'unaffiliated' scribbled in black marker on the front of it. I couldn't help but laugh out loud, and remarked to my wife, "There is no way this guy isn't former SOF, hell, I bet he used to be a Ranger!"

I shared the picture, thinking it was hilarious and that the world needed to know about this man. About a day later, a friend of mine, Iassen Donov of 3rd Ranger Battalion fame, commented that he was actually his roommate, and yes, he was a Ranger. I guess we can always tell our own! It wasn't much later when Leo and I connected via Facebook, me asking if he would write something for a book I was working on, and would he agree to be sponsored by my brand new company, *Blackside Concepts*? He, of course, agreed, and that was the beginning of what would become a great friendship and business partnership that would see us traveling the globe less than two years later.

Little did I know back then, that at that very competition, he was struggling. Not athletically, but beneath the beard and tattoos. He was a fellow Ranger Buddy who was still in the midst of a transition from military service that I had yet to even begin at the time. Isn't that how it always works out though? We never seem to know our fellow brothers and sisters-in-arms are struggling. At least twenty-two times a day, we don't find out until it is too late. We don't try to understand until it's... too late.

What I also didn't know back then, is that Leo Jenkins would become an agent of change. Someone who would go on to champion veterans transition issues, to spread awareness, and even talk good men out of very bad situations. Little did I know that he would abandon a beachfront paradise in Costa Rica to become a homeless transient in the hopes of contributing to the cause. Little did I know he would tear open the scabs on his internal wounds to write possibly the most important book ever written on veterans and their transition from the military to civilian life.

With less than one half of one percent of the total population serving at any given time, there is a large gap in understanding the challenges our warrior-elite face. For the 88% of America (and increasing) who have never put on a uniform, our challenges are largely out of sight and out of mind. Every time a tragedy or security situation arises somewhere in the world, America cries out for "someone" to do "something." That someone is usually the American service member, and that something usually involves them going into harm's way and doing things few others can or will do. Yet very little thought is ever given to how we help those same service members come back home. This book shows exactly what one can, and often time does, endure in an attempt to help themselves in that process. This book gives you the inside look at exactly what happens after "someone" does "something" and then has to attempt a return to "normal."

As you read through this book, I beg that you not read the words with pity for Leo. His story is certainly compelling, and at times you may be angered or saddened by the situations he has found himself in. I beg that you not read this with pity for veterans as a whole either. Pity is not what we need. What we need is to be seen as people who are not so different than most of the rest of America, but with different experiences. Some of us went to basic training instead of freshman orientation after high school. Some of us went to an officer candidate board instead of an internship interview after college. Some of us endured combat deployments instead of semesters abroad. Certainly they are different experiences, and different paths. But one demographic has to deal with the stigma of PTSD when interviewing for a job whether they have it or not. They have to water down their resume in the hopes that the HR manager will understand it. What do we need? To be seen as equals, and given a fair shake. For those who need help or rehabilitation to be given what they were promised would be there for them.

America wants us to leave the military and seamlessly assimilate back into society as if that part of our life never happened. They don't want to hear about the son who asks you if his father is dead. They don't want to hear about how you told him his daddy was fine, and please be quiet, even though minute's prior, you stepped over the fragments of his father's skull, and the contents it once protected. They don't want to hear about how we sat in plywood boxes, sweating through our uniform for a ten-minute call with our loved ones. A ten minute call that would conclude with an obligatory, "I love you, talk to you soon" – even though we knew the latter was a potential lie.

What I would ask is that you give this book to someone who doesn't know any veterans, who is consumed by their "first world" problems, problems afforded to them on behalf of generation after generation of an ever shrinking warrior class, and ask them to meet us half way. Try to understand our background and our veteran community as much as we try to return to 'normal' – despite all the challenges some of us face when trying to do so.

-Marty Skovlund, Jr.
CEO, Blackside Concepts

Author's Preface

I am going to be honest with you because I feel like you deserve that. I am not an author. I am not an academic. I don't have a wall full of degrees that make me a subject matter expert in the sociology of assimilation. I have attempted to write a flowery introduction to this book several times. Each version more flush with six dollar words than the one before it. Each one further removed from the point and increasingly pompous in its own right. That, however, is not who I am.

    At twenty years old, blinded by a cloud of animosity created by the falling rubble of the attack on the World Trade Center, I enlisted in the U.S. Army as a medic. I would go on to graduate the US Special Operations Medical Course (SOMC) and operate as a member of 3rd Ranger Battalion through multiple combat deployments in support America's role in the global war on terrorism. The combat experiences that have led to the following work have been recorded in my first book, *Lest We Forget: A Ranger Medic's Story*.

What follows is an account of the tribulations associated with leaving the military and attempting to reintegrate myself back into society. In my search for insight on this subject, I discovered that the overwhelming majority of books written on related topics have been composed by people with a PhD in psychology, who have never been in the military, let alone deployed to combat. While I appreciate the effort they have dedicated to bringing these issues to the forefront, I believe that they are lacking a certain amount of grit necessary to effectively tell the story.

This book can be read as a memoir; however, it is more intended to pose certain questions regarding the psychological effects of returning from war than it is to tell a story. It is my experience that the vast majority of veterans do not desire to reopen the scars that they incurred during war. Many will not discuss such vicissitude due to the emotional pain that accompanies recalling. Following the release of my first book, I was taken aback by the number of men who, upon reading it, passed it on to family members and friends saying, "I know that I don't talk about what I went through, but this book comes pretty damn close to my experience if you are curious." With that, my words were able to transcend to become theirs and I was able to be a voice for those who had difficulty telling their story. To say that I was honored to be in such a position would be a grave understatement.

First and foremost, my hope is that any veteran who has felt alone in their journey back into the civilian world will realize that they are the furthest thing from it, that the majority of service members leaving the military face similar perils and often feel secluded in the solitude of a crowded room.

My second intention is to show how I could have better prepared for and approached this transition. As you will see, I believe that finding meaningful employment is one of the most important aspects to making a successful transition from the military to the civilian sector. The training that members of the military obtain is often second to none yet can be overlooked due to the way in which it is presented.

It would be difficult to argue that our government is doing everything possible to assist our combat veterans in their assimilation. With over twenty veterans a day deciding to take their own life, a life that they once used to protect our nation, much more can be done. It has become apparent to me at this point that many of those tasked with easing this transition just do not understand it.

I hope with all of my heart that the words that follow act as a window into a world that less than a half of a percent of our population actually lives in. However, the onus is not on the government alone. It is up to each and every one of us, veteran and civilian alike, to shoulder our share of the task. Just because I fought does not exclude me from the responsibility of helping others that have. This is not a textbook; I am not an educated man. I am a war fighter. This is real. This is a Ranger medic's return from war.

x

Introduction

In a coffee shop in north Denver, as the snow flurries swirl and dance and hang in the air, I reflect on my military service and the seven years since that has brought me to this place. Not just my physical residence but my mental state and the way in which I see the world and the people in it. I look to the happy couple that just walked in with a degree of antipathy. Why is that? They seem like nice people, but a part of me holds them in disdain. Maybe it isn't antipathy at all, perhaps it is jealousy or envy that is coursing through my veins. I allow my mind to wonder what it would be like to be rid of the ghosts and guilt of two wars. A weight that neither in this pair could ever understand.

I find myself clinging to a world that I have long since left. October 20th, 2006, a date that will forever be ingrained in my memory. 20OCT2006 was the day that I went from being an Army Ranger, to being a veteran. Over 2,500 sunrises have come and gone since that day, nearly twice the number that came and went during my time as a soldier. Yet somehow there is still a feeling residing in me that identifies more with the clean-shaven, beret-wearing version of me. I can't let him go. He is the best version of me that I have ever known.

Every one of those 2,500+ days I have attempted to reintegrate into our social fabric so that I may be accepted back into a society that does not understand my disposition. This is not solely my struggle; this is the plight of millions of veterans today who find themselves adrift to some degree.

It is important not to confuse struggle with ineffectiveness, for these are the most capable individuals of our generation. Their struggle lay not in inability, but rather in being a minority who has supported a majority. Their struggle is the perceived under-appreciation for a donation of their most fruitful years. A struggle for which the most well adjusted veteran is underprepared. It is the greatest battle that most will never face, an ongoing endeavor to achieve an internal expectation, one put in place by an experience that few will ever know. Our process of rejoining the masses is currently our burden to bear. It is our greatest mission. It is our albatross. The last long walk of our enlistment is our assimilation and an arduous one it is.

Long hours, bad food, and inadequate pay are staples of military service. Being shot at and placed in situations where you are required to take the life of another human being are merely a part of the job description. Watching your nieces, nephews, sons, and daughters grow up in pictures from half a world away, no doubt pulls on the heart strings of the most battle hardened soldier. I can say now with utmost confidence, however, that the most difficult part of wearing that uniform is hanging it up. The process of assimilation is long and convoluted. The physical, mental, and emotional demands placed on most members of the military far exceed their civilian counterparts, yet for some reason the same professional courtesies do not typically extend to those who have donned camouflage. College level courses, as well as professional certifications achieved in the military, seldom transfer to a civilian equivalent.

This is not an attempt at glorifying military service or an effort to create an atmosphere of pity; neither would be helpful to veterans. The military is a voluntary path and although most people don't have a comprehensive understanding of what they will inevitably experience upon enlisting, it is a path that is chosen with free will. That does not, however, mean that the burdens of this profession should be shouldered solely by those in uniform. We all have a social responsibility to understand those who have sacrificed so much for our way of life. Your ideological ethos does not have to be in line with those who serve, but you absolutely have a social obligation to understand the trials and tribulations that they endured for your benefit. The days of, "I don't want to know what happens over there," and, "hearing about it makes me feel uncomfortable," are over.

The difficulty transitioning from the military world into civilian life is multifaceted. There is a very structured, systematic progression in taking a civilian and turning them into a soldier. Step by step, day after day, through the course of basic training soldiers are taught how to conduct tasks in a very specific manner. They are not only taught the proper way of making their bed and shining their boots, they are held accountable by their peers and superiors alike if these tasks are not completed to standard. There is no equivalent to this upon discharge. Anyone that has ever attempted to quit anything cold turkey understands that it can often be an ineffective technique. A few hours of briefings and resume classes do not make up for months and years of institutionalized indoctrination. It isn't that a veteran doesn't know how to think for himself; the problem is that they have been a critical member of a team for years. They had a specific role to play and when that role is so drastically altered, finding yourself can be difficult.

Following release from the military, new veterans lose the most significant support group that they have ever known. The simple truth is that the only people who will ever understand the demons experienced in battle are the ones standing by your side when those demons made their grand entrance. There is no need to express to those men how you are feeling regarding those events because they feel the same way. There is more comfort in that than you can possibly imagine. To go from being surrounded by a group of people who relate on the most intimate level to being isolated from every one of them overnight is a highly traumatic event that often isn't even recognized. This particular moment is disguised by the jubilee of being free from the perceived oppression of the military itself. That oppression, in hindsight, is actually the extension of the most caring extended family a person can know.

As a soldier, in order to accomplish the required tasks of your profession you must possess the highest degree of confidence. When returning to civilian life, the same confidence that has served to keep you alive in an austere environment is looked upon as an unnecessary arrogance. It is the service member who is forced to adapt to the outlook of the popular majority in this situation. This becomes an initial source of animosity; why should the veteran be made to conform to the parts of society that sat back when there was work to do? One of the most fundamental and problematic aspects of assimilation for military veterans is quite simply a misunderstanding on the part of civilians perpetrated by movies and television. Films featuring veterans seem to go one of two ways. They are either an emotionless, unfeeling death machine or so completely broken by their experience that they are a danger to society. It is a sad, simple truth that the way the media depicts military life is largely inaccurate. Yet this, not reality, is how most civilians form their opinions of members of the armed services.

We leave a world of black and white, wrongs and rights, to join a world of endless shades of gray, one where standing orders no longer dictate daily activities and people do not live by a creed. Morals are contorted to serve the individual rather than the greater good of the group. Many veterans step off a train upon leaving the military and set out on a journey with no designated path. That train that they grew accustomed to was perpetually on a very calculated route. Something as simple as, "should I get a haircut today?" is a choice that was predetermined by a mandate.

The following story attempts to portray those tribulations through my own personal experiences. This story depicts the journey of leaving the safe comforts of war and returning to the harsh realities of civilian society. From the conversations I have had with hundreds of other veterans I have discovered that I was not the only one to experience these issues, deal with these fears and dance with these demons. I learned that I am not alone. I had for years, however, been under the impression that such things should not impact a strong man. I watched men that I admire carry on with what seemed like indifference to the same events that at times crippled my mind, never knowing that they too were being strangled by the same monster.

Chapter 1: A Departure

"Agggggghhhhhhhh" The suppressed guttural scream escaped my lungs. How long had I been holding that in? Years, I suppose. All of the stress and pressure of my job had been compiling itself on my shoulders for what felt like a lifetime and now, just like that, it was gone.

As I pulled away from the uninviting, eight-foot tall brown fence adorned with weathered barbed wire that separated 3rd Ranger Battalion from the rest of the world, a wave of unbridled expansive freedom crashed over me. For several years, I was made to ask permission if I wanted to go anywhere. Forms had to be filled out requesting endorsement for any type of travel; an ironic notion in and of itself when you consider that one of the purposes of the US service member is to maintain the ability of its nation's citizens to travel uninhibited, without restriction from government. Upon enlistment, a certain percentage of your rights are relinquished in an effort to secure those of the majority. It's a necessary evil, one that we all accept. Now, for the first time, I could go anywhere without asking permission from another human being. The choice was now mine to shave or not to shave, to sleep in or wake up early. The decision and subsequent destination of travel was mine to make.

I had been responsible for the health and well being of the warriors of Charlie Company for years. Treating small scrapes or gunshot wounds, maintaining shot records or prescribing drugs, it was all my responsibility. Now I wasn't responsible for anything. Just like that, I was released from the willful obligation of taking care of my fellow Rangers: my best friends, my brothers.

It was an uncommonly warm day for late October, as if the sun had come out to see me off. The sun seemed to be the only one who did. There was no party, no ceremony, and no fuss. To be honest, I preferred it that way. I have never liked saying goodbye; I have never had a problem leaving a place. Yet, for some reason, it felt as though I had cleaved a part of myself off and left it behind that brown fence. As much as it may seem like the military will cease in your absence, it somehow finds a way to go on without you. The day I left, Charlie Company was preparing for yet another long day of training; the mission goes on in your absence regardless of how important your role was.

I glanced at the tan beret staring back at me from the dash of my pickup truck. It was impossible to not reflect on all that I had sacrificed to obtain and keep that piece of headgear. On the first day of the selection process to become a Ranger, I vowed that I would rather die than go home without it. Every day for years, I fought to maintain the standards of my Ranger Regiment so that it would not be taken from me. It was a symbol that told a story of generations of honorable men. It was as respected as it was coveted among those in uniform. Accelerating off of Fort Benning and into the unknown of what the future held, I knew I would never again don that beret in an official capacity. It simultaneously filled me with the excitement of future possibility and broke my heart.

I was the first one home that day. I shared a house off of exit six with Nicky P., Morty, and Graves, all fellow Rangers from Charlie Company. My good friend Matt Voll had recently been honorably discharged from the Ranger Regiment and moved out of the large house that we all lived in and headed back to the Midwest. We had spent our early twenties together not even knowing how unique the bond that we had created was.

With the force of a wrecking ball, my dog Jameson smashed into my leg as I entered the front door. The little, brown pit-mix was still in her awkward puppy phase. Just a few months before the house felt so empty. On one of my last missions in Iraq, I tore a hole in my abdominal wall and had to return to the US for surgery. Maybe it was the hot summer nights in Georgia, or maybe it was knowing that the men that I loved were still deployed while I was safe, but either way I wasn't sleeping much in those days.

Conducting multiple direct action raids on different high value targets in a single evening was
routine during my final deployment. Several members of our platoon felt the sting of a suicide bomber from a range that should have vaporized their existence into little more than pink mist. Bullets from a PKM machine gun ruined the helmet of one of our fire team members. Helicopter crashes sent men into rescue mode and firefights that illuminated the hot, vast Mesopotamian night with green beams of infrared light emitted from the PEQ-2 lasers affixed to our M4 assault rifles were a regular occurrence.

It was the kind of deployment that most Rangers dream about, nonstop action that tested the
skills we had spent years refining. Roughly 100 direct action missions in 90 days, at the end of which, every member from our task force returned home to their families. A statistic that the enemy could not boast as our platoon alone was responsible for the eradication of dozens of known bomb makers, foreign fighters, and jihadists in that time span. It becomes easy to accept that you may lose your life during those times, so much so that about two months into that deployment I actually wrote my own eulogy.

Thirty years old seemed as far away to me as one hundred and thirty does to most people. I had come to terms with the fact that I would not see my third decade of life. What I could not so easily accept was the loss of a brother. My primary purpose as a Ranger medic was to ensure the return of each of my men. My life was for the preservation of theirs and I swear to this day, if given the chance, I would have gladly forfeited mine for any one of theirs. So when I had to return to the States while those men sat in harm's way, it dismantled me. With the intimate knowledge of the timelines which they operated, I knew almost to the minute when they were boarding the Black Hawk helicopters on the airstrip behind our compound in Iraq. I knew when they were on target and how tired they were. I knew the extreme danger that they continued to face despite my absence. It is possible that in those days I felt what my father must have gone through watching me depart for such a place, what every parent or spouse must go through. I had 38 brothers simultaneously deployed and no bullshit story about how, "all we do is play video games and workout" was going to pass as truth. I knew better.

When I returned from Iraq alone, it was suggested by a doctor on post that I should get a dog. Following my surgery, she laid by my side for almost an entire week providing me with comfort during a very uncomfortable time. She seemed to be there for me the way that my Ranger brothers would have been if they could have. That kind of relationship is rare. That level of commitment isn't as common as I wish it was.

It had only been a few months since I got her but she had already grown so much. When I returned home from my final day as a Ranger, Jameson knew that something was going on. The moving boxes created a sort of controlled chaos throughout the house. It is amazing how dogs can just sense that something is about to change. Omitting a slight grunt of discomfort from the still-healing mesh screen holding my abdominal wall together, I bent over to pick her up. Responding the way that puppies often do, she excitedly urinated all down the front of my Army Combat Uniform. On any other day I may have been upset, but what did I care? I would never have to put that uncomfortable hideous excuse of a uniform on ever again.

It took fewer than 48 hours to pack everything that I owned and load it in the back of my old Dodge pickup. It took another 31 hours to make the drive from Columbus, Georgia back to Phoenix. I couldn't get away from that place fast enough. There was nothing for me there anymore and I was eager to see my family again. If my truck had not been packed to the gills with all of my earthly possessions, it would have been impossible to resist the desire to turn left into Juarez, Mexico as I passed through El Paso. At that point, I had been awake for well over 24 hours and Jameson didn't look like she had any desire to make a pit stop in another country so we pressed on. A quick 20-minute nap in New Mexico and the drive continued. The cross-country trek may have seemed arduous if I hadn't been so excited about the new chapter unfolding before me.

I had a vague outline of what I wanted to do once I arrived in Phoenix, but it lacked the structure that I had become accustomed to. The first order of business was to connect with old friends and simply get caught up with what had occurred in the lives of my family members since I had left. For the most part, I was going to just show up and figure it out as life came at me.

I surprised everyone when I arrived two days early. I had just thrown myself back into the mix. Most people take for granted the nature of their family dynamic as something that inherently exists. However, in your absence that nucleus tends to evolve without your influence. The experiences that define us are difficult to share with people void of a similar history with any reasonable hope of comprehension. I just lived a lifetime in the matter of a few years; the wedge that is created as a result, fissure-like. During my time in the military, I formed a new family, a group of brothers that became intimately familiar with my personality and I with theirs. Despite knowing how much my family had always supported me there was still a certain level of anxiety associated with trying to find my place among them once again.

I was very fortunate to have a family who understood that I would be dancing with demons. I had a father and siblings to come home to, but no one whom I was truly responsible for. I cannot imagine the throes that afflicted those men whose small children didn't even recognize them upon their return home. Even though my family had empathy for me and were pleased when I returned, they had no understanding of the circumstances that now separated us. Simultaneously, they had all grown during their own journey, and I was now back piecing together their stories. We were still very much a family; however, my association with that nucleus had been strained by years devoid of physical and emotional connection.

What I had wasn't really a plan, but more the absence of a plan. I knew I wanted to attend school while trying to get hired by the Peoria Fire Department, but I didn't know what I wanted to study or what my approach would be for testing for the municipality. It felt good to be free though. So much so that I wasn't really thinking much about how I would manage my future. The rest is in the fine print, as they say.

Within days of arriving back home in Arizona, I found myself basking in the sting of wind and sun in the middle of the desert, on my way to Mexico atop my Harley Davidson with my father on his by my side. After my first deployment, I talked him into teaching me how to drive a motorcycle. Then on the same day, I convinced him that we should ride to Las Vegas. To this day, I am still surprised that he agreed to that trip. On another visit home, we found ourselves cruising through San Diego and eventually in Tijuana for a splash of tequila and a few cow tongue tacos.

I had my own Harley now and I wanted to see if it could keep up with his Road King. We cracked the silence of the vast open desert air; like a gang of cowboys galloping on steel horses, a pack of firefighters my dad and I rolled south toward Mexico. Hundreds of riders were meeting in the small beach town of Puerto Penasco for a motorcycle rally with a bit of international flare. The experience was surreal for me. I went where I wanted, when I wanted, without asking permission.

My father's buddies owned a house in Cholla Bay. The house was small but nice, more importantly it was a very short walk to JJ's Cantina. If you've never gone beer-drinking with a group of firefighters, I strongly suggest adding it to your list of things to do. They made sure I didn't pay for a drink the entire time. Sitting at the bar, we overheard that a massive house party with an open bar and a very popular Phoenix band called, Mogollon was popping off nearby. The discussion on if we should crash the party was quite short. The house was easy to find, it was illuminated like a Christmas tree in an otherwise dark neighborhood. The band had just started playing in the backyard as we confidently made entry through the front door. I followed Mike's lead as we strutted through the mini mansion. Most of the crowd had gathered in the back yard to take in the classic rock music that was being performed with an ocean back drop.

As soon as we made it to the back patio, my eyes fixated on two targets simultaneously, the giant trough filled with beer and the tall brunette standing next to it. "Can I buy you a drink?" I joked to her as I pulled two Tecates from the ice filled bucket. She laughed. That's good, she thinks I'm funny. Naturally, I am funny. "You come here often?" I slurred in a cheesy joking manner.

"To Mexico?"

"No, here, to this house."

"Umm no, I've never been here before. Who are you?"

"That's not really important. You wanna find the bar and do some shots?"

"Haha, maybe later."

After finding the fully stocked bar, I returned with two shots of tequila. "Look, I know that no really means yes so I brought you one anyway."

Mike, and the rest of the firemen just laughed at me as she stormed off in a slightly disgusted manner.

"Not sure what her deal is, I wish someone would bring me free booze and make a rape joke to me!" I yelled at the guys over the loud music as I slammed back both shots and reached back into the beer bucket for another cold one. The rest of the night was a bit hazy. I blacked out and when I came to I was teaching the guys how to clear a house, citing hazard points like the fatal funnel and ensuring that everyone knew which corner they should be flowing to. To this day, I'm still not sure whose house it was we used as our shoot house. The next morning I was discovered by one of the firemen's wives asleep on the front porch, utilizing a bath towel as a blanket. When she kindly attempted to trade out the towel for a blanket, I was startled awake, brandishing the knife that I had been clenching in my right hand while I slept.

I noticed a golf cart pulled up to the front entrance of the house. "Where the hell did that come from?" I mumbled, attempting to not disrupt my hangover. "Hahaha, you don't remember stealing that from JJ's last night?"

"What? No, we left JJ's at like nine to go to that party."

"Yeah, then we went back."

"Oh shit! Really."

In his typical fatherly voice my dad chimed in, "Leo, what the fuck did you do last night?"

"Bruce, what happens in Mexico, stays in Mexico." Mike replied with a smile that not even his giant black mustache could cover.

The time in Mexico afforded me the opportunity to begin to reflect on my years of service. I had been going so hard for so long that I never really had the chance to stop and absorb all that had occurred. That moment was about me, whereas the years prior were not. It was a necessary moment of selfishness. One which inadvertently opened a Pandora's Box of memories. Combat is fast. There is no time to stop and think about the repercussions of the events that are occurring, if you do, you die. If you let those moments seep in during training you become less effective. As a result, they are stowed away, pushed back into a compartment in your mind to be dealt with on a latter day. Little did I know that day was upon me.

Chapter 2: Edit Your Hometown

When we returned from the long weekend trip, reality began to set in. I was going to have to figure out how to live without the military while simultaneously managing the new onslaught of emotions related to my time in service. I was very fortunate that my younger sister, Ashley, had a modest four-bedroom condo that she was living in by herself. It was actually the same place that we grew up in together. My father still owned and rented it to her at a "fatherly price." I had informed her prior to arriving in Arizona that I would be taking one of the rooms and that she didn't have a choice. We always had that kind of relationship. We fought as children the way that siblings often do but became the best of friends as adults. If this place had not existed, I could have very easily ended up homeless. I didn't have the money when I got out to afford a place of my own, and since I had no job, very few places, if any, would have rented an apartment to me.

Ashley worked as a stylist at a salon in Glendale. I had felt terrible about missing so much of my family's lives over the years. I had this opportunity to make up for that fact so I spent a great deal of time loitering at her place of business. The fact that the staff and patrons alike were attractive females, a population that I had been all but removed from over the past four years, never made the decision to visit difficult.

After a couple of weeks of pestering the staff of the salon, the tall blonde receptionist covered in tattoos failed to show up for work one afternoon. The owner of the establishment made a passing joke to me, "Leo, since you're here so much, why don't you just start answering the phones?" I'm sure she regretted the jest when she entered her business the next morning to the sight of yours truly standing behind the front desk making a reservation over the phone. Her eyes expanded to double their previous size as she loudly whispered through clenched teeth, "What are you doing?"

"Please hold." I asked of the nice women on the phone. I reminded her of her comment the day before and she hesitantly agreed to pay me to answer the phones until she could find a more appropriate employee.

I went from conducting high profile special operations missions to folding towels and sweeping up hair. I adapted to the task well. I never did claim the $150 I made that week to the IRS, but I could now add "Salon Receptionist" to my resume right after the title "Army Ranger." Though it was a small one, it was a step in the right direction. I was able to reconnect with my little sister while showing that I could complete tasks outside of performing surgical procedures in the dark of night. Despite how quickly I adapted to the task I was replaced by a more suitable candidate. Being replaced by a seventeen-year-old girl could have been looked at as a set back or insult, but at the time I had the utmost confidence that I would have no trouble finding a real job that I just laughed it off.

Aside from going back to school at the end of January, I didn't have a plan for how I was going to support myself. This was the primary mistake that I made when I left the service. Every day in Ranger Battalion was planned out. What kind of training we would be conducting, with whom, and for how long. I never thought about how accustomed to that structure I had become during my time behind that brown fence. I knew that I worked hard every day and was a person that could be depended on when a job became difficult. For some reason I figured that would be enough to entice a potential employer to hire me immediately.

I had intended to work for the fire department but this process can take years to accomplish. There is a physical agility test, a written exam, multiple oral board interviews, and psychological screenings. It had taken my father five years to navigate the process, however, in my mind it would be much faster for me to get hired. I assumed that any number of businesses would fight for the opportunity to have someone with my credentials working for them. I composed my resume with my work history and accomplishments. I was only twenty four but had already done so much.

I started off applying at local bars and restaurants. I had worked as a bar back and bus boy for three years as a teenager and so figured that a job waiting tables would be perfect while I was testing for the fire department. I applied at every one of the twenty restaurants within a four mile radius. When none of them called back, I expanded to an eight mile radius. After a couple of weeks without a call, I decided to be more proactive and follow up in person

A large bar and grille had just been built a few miles away and was hiring for every position. I had already submitted an application, when I didn't hear back I took it upon myself to create an interview opportunity. I arrived to the brand new establishment in the middle of the afternoon on a Tuesday. The kitchen staff had recently been hired and was being taken through training. When I asked to speak to a manager regarding an application that I recently submitted, I received an odd look, one that suggested *we didn't call you, what are you doing here?*

After about a twenty minute wait, a young man my age invited me to sit with him at one of the booths.

"Leo, is it?"

"Yes sir. Thank you for taking the time to see me"

"Well I have your application here. It says that you were a medic in the Army and before that you were a firefighter and EMT. It looks like you worked as a bus boy quite some time ago. Have you ever served before?"

"Well, I served my country. Does that count?" I joked.

"I meant tables. Have you ever waited tables? It can get pretty stressful at times." *Is he joking right now? Maybe he is responding to my joke with a joke of his own. Laugh at your future bosses stupid joke, idiot!*

"HAHAHAHA!"

"What's funny about that?" *Ohh shit! He wasn't joking! He is holding my application that says that my last job was a decorated Ranger medic and is talking to me about the stress of pouring tea in someone's Pepsi by mistake.*

The interview concluded with the obligatory, "We'll give you a call."

I wish I could say that the next dozen places that I showed up to went better but they didn't. I found out very quickly that very few civilian employers care how many Special Operations courses you have passed or how many men you were responsible for providing care for. Most of that stemmed from a complete ignorance. Over the course of my first six months post-military, I had submitted a resume or application at approximately 160 different organizations ranging from the fire department to bars and restaurants to Jamba Juice. The overwhelming majority of people in a hiring position had no clue regarding the capabilities of a member of Special Operations or even the military as a whole.

I've listened to human resource managers of major companies speak on how highlighting your military service on an application is actually detrimental to being hired in many places. Even if I had been privy to this insight in late 2006, it wouldn't have mattered. The pride I felt in all that I had accomplished far outweighed my willingness to conform to what would be appealing to someone in human resources. After all, they hadn't done what I had done; they had no idea what hard work was or all that I was capable of!

I highlighted my service because I saw the value in it, even if they didn't. I saw myself as a candidate who would always be fifteen minutes early and work until my hands bled. I saw myself as a person who understood the chain of command and was task oriented. It wasn't my shortcoming that the people responsible for staffing their ranks couldn't see those attributes. The fact that I was still making up for so many of the experiences that most Americans in their early twenties take for granted, made things even more toilsome. I was trying to catch up on all the things that I felt like I missed while being away.

I did find a few temporary part-time jobs in the first few months after my departure. One of the firefighters who had worked with my father for years, named Robert Brewster, offered me part time work assisting him with his side business, most of which was plumbing work that I had absolutely no clue how to do. Robert taught me just enough basic skills so I wouldn't glue my hands together. I showed up early and stayed late. I took direction from Robert as though I was being given orders from a platoon sergeant. It gave me someplace to be and a little money in my pocket but the work was inconsistent. I am eternally grateful for the couple of weeks of work that he had for me and the skills that I learned during that time. Following so many rejections, it reminded me that I was a highly capable person. Sure I didn't know anything about plumbing, but the military had taught me how to be a fast learner.

I found another part time job to supplement my income as a bouncer at a local club. It had been about six weeks since I got out and I had my first steady job.

Sort of. I was making eight dollars an hour, working twelve hours a week. After taxes, I was taking home an impressive four thousand dollars a year. It wasn't enough to pay for the utility bills in Phoenix, let alone rent.

I was absolutely blessed to be able to have a place to stay for free and an old pick up and motorcycle that had been paid off after my last trip to Iraq. Tens of thousands of veterans don't have that advantage. If it had not been for the support of my family during this time, I could have easily ended up sleeping on the streets the way over 60,000 other military veterans are this very evening. Although even with their support, the financial burden began to mount.

Christmas was just days away and I couldn't afford to buy a single gift for the people who had supported me through so much already. Sitting on my father's couch, I watched as all of my young nieces and nephews opened gifts from their other uncles and aunts. I'm not sure if I have ever felt as worthless as I did on that moment. I didn't want to open any of the gifts that lay at my feet. Everyone in the room laughed and exchanged gifts and all I wanted to do was crawl into a hole. The closest thing I could find was a bottle of whiskey on the top shelf of my father's pantry. I didn't care that it was 10 AM on Christmas morning. I didn't care at all. The unbearable sting of inadequacy and impotence could, in that moment, only be squelched by the sweet soft indulgence of a tall glass of scotch. An outcry, to the lost dreams and sense of wonder, to the streets that raised me. I began to say goodbye to the hope for the home I'd been holding.

In just two short months, I went from serving in one of the most altruistic roles that our nation employs, that of a Special Operations Medic, to being the drunk uncle at Christmas. My appearance was unkempt and I didn't care. I was disgruntled and alone with nothing to give. I didn't always love my job in the military but every single day I woke up with the greatest sense of purpose imaginable. No matter how long the hours, or terrible the food, or lousy the pay, I knew in my heart that I was serving something bigger than myself. My life's work was to ensure that each of the men in my care came home that they may live on and be purposeful and impact the lives of those whom they encountered. Now I had no purpose. I had no band of brothers to lean on, and more importantly, I didn't have them leaning on me. Without purpose, responsibility, or the respect of dozens of hiring managers who refused to return my calls, I plummeted into what I have come to know as "my downward spiral."

Chapter 3: The Most Beautiful Bitter Fruit

I didn't recognize it as a problem when I was taking three to four shots of whiskey before hopping on my Street Bob and zipping down the road at eighty miles an hour to get to my job checking IDs at the club. When the effects of the Jameson wore off too fast, I began filling 20oz water bottles with Everclear and taking them with me to work. In four hours I could easily finish one straight. As the days progressed my sense of worth decreased and my need to numb myself increased. Comments from one of the overweight bouncers that I was working with echoed in my head. "How long does it take to get your shit together after the military, really? I mean you were a civilian for what, like twenty years then a soldier for four? What the fuck is with you guys? Get over it!"

I felt like a foreign object in a host body and every effort was being made to encapsulate and push me out. I wasn't a positive force in this organism; I was a cancer to it. Since most of my friends were bartenders or servers, they would be getting off work about the same time that I was. Once again, I would crack the pipes of my six speed, matte black bobber through the streets of Peoria, Arizona, at close to 100 miles an hour to I meet up with my friends. We frequently sat around a backyard fire and drank until the sun came up. I would pass out for an hour or two and then head to the gym where I would spend hours physically punishing myself into a state of exhaustion. After sundown, before sleeping, I was the worst of me. A mess of these old themes and the murmur of half-dreams whispered seductively. The emotional pain of feeling completely worthless was only mitigated by copious amounts of alcohol or extreme physical fatigue. The barbell and the bottle became my therapists.

Waking up in mid-January, after the bar's holiday party, I found my skull stuck to the sheets of my bed. As I gave the light blue linen a tug, I realized that blood from an open wound on the back of my head was acting as the adhesive. The pieces of the previous evening flashed in my mind as I attempted to sit up. Pulling the dried chunks of vomit from my beard, I began vaguely recalling riding to the party standing on the roof of my friend's truck with a bottle of vodka in my hand. Did I fall off the roof of his house? I did. What was I doing up there? I landed on his grill. Fuck I broke my boss' barbeque grill with my head. The room spun like a merry-go-round possessed as I tried to remember how I even got home.

By this time, my former Battalion had just left for their next rotation overseas. Just like before, when I had to return from Iraq for surgery, I knew exactly when they were in harm's way. If I was at the gym in Arizona, I knew at that time of day they were most likely getting ready to set a demo breach on a door and run head first into the mouth of the beast. I should have been there with them. I jumped at the opportunity to be with my family and in turn walked away from the men who had been my brothers for years.

When I left for the military, I was excited but at the same time thought about my family and how they would respond to my absence. These thoughts consumed me even prior to my departure for basic training. As a result, I made a plan for how I would maintain communication with them. Twice a week, I would sit down and write a letter to a different member of my family while I was in basic training. As soon as I received phone privileges, I called every chance that I could. It was paramount to my identity that I maintained those relationships as best as I could. Yet for some reason, I didn't do the same thing when I left my brothers in Georgia. I just walked out one day. I just abandoned them. A part of me wanted to forget about that place so I ran from it. I confused moving forward to a new chapter in my life with running away from a place that shaped the foundation of my character.

It became important to fill the void I was beginning to feel with something meaningful. I had never in my life run more than ten miles and decided abruptly that I wanted to run a half marathon.

Remembering how much fun it was to compete in my first triathlon with my father prior to enlisting in the Army, I challenged him to run the 13.1 miles with me. He made the mistake of agreeing to the event without asking any other questions. The look on his face when I told him that the race was only two weeks away and at a much higher altitude was priceless. I had to repeat, "You already said you would!" over and over as he shook his head. To his credit, he stayed true to his word. With little to no proper training, we set out early on that chilly Saturday morning, up into the mountains of Northern Arizona.

My father has always been my role model, not because he possesses some superhuman athletic ability, or is wealthy, or for any other superficial reason. It's because he does what he says he is going to do and because he does it with a light-hearted, jovial attitude. In life there will always be things that we have to do that we don't want to do, the only real control we have is how we respond to those moments. My father always seems to respond with a smile. So even when he crossed the finish line, feet bleeding, completely out of sweat and exhausted, he did it with a smile.

That to me has always been the reason for suffering through the various crucibles of the military. When you arrive, victorious and graduated from the obstacles that have been placed before you, in whatever selection or training completed, you know that the person standing next to you will not capitulate when things become difficult. You know that you can count on those individuals being there when things become difficult again. That is what makes them family. On this particular day, I felt blessed to have two different families that would suffer and stand for me.

Laughing and enjoying a cup of coffee on the long drive back to Peoria, my father and I laughed about how bad that run sucked. He joked with me about finding the woman with the nicest ass to run behind for motivation and that he may not have finished if it wasn't for her. "God bless her... and those shorts she was wearing." He chuckled. At that moment, my cell phone vibrated across the dash of my dad's extended cab white Chevy pick-up. As I glanced at the caller ID, I noticed it was one of my good friends from Ranger Battalion. "What's up brother?"

"Hey Doc, what's up?"

"Ohh, just got done running a half marathon with my dad with no training. Haha! No big deal."

"Hey brother, I'm going to keep this short because I don't have much information yet, but Jimmy Regan is dead."

The cable was cut on the elevator that I had been riding to the top floor all morning. My heart somehow became lodged in my throat and had I not already been sitting down my knees surely would have buckled beneath the force of impact that one sentence had made.

"What? How? When?"

"I don't have many details right now Doc, but I will let you know when I do. Congrats on the race, brother."

How dare I be as happy as I just was? Here I am laughing and joking about chasing women while my friends were dying.

In three combat deployments as a Ranger medic not one of my men died. The first deployment after my departure, a deployment that I should have been on, a man who I was at one time responsible for had his final day. On February 9th, 2007, my friend and fellow Ranger, Sergeant James Regan was killed by a roadside bomb. Now you can say that there was nothing I could have done and today I would believe you, but if you tried to feed me that line in February of 2007 there would have been a good chance that I would have broken every bone in your face.

A painful amalgam of helplessness, resentment, self-loathing, and alcohol abuse completely consumed me. It was an all-consuming, crippling type of pain. I didn't get out of bed for nearly four days following that race with my father. Every possible scenario of how he could have died cycled through my mind as I stared at the ceiling, unblinking. I thought of what I could have done. The weight of my failed responsibility sat heavy on my chest, pinning me to the bed beneath me. I really didn't care if I lived anymore. If I had access to a gun at that point in my life, I would likely not be here writing this today. It was as if someone had my soul by the throat and was choking it without mercy. The guilt I had over James' death was not my burden, yet I shouldered it as though it was that massive old green rucksack that I had become all too familiar with in previous years. My purpose was for him and men like him; now I was without that purpose. My hands were bound with razor wire and I was tossed to bob adrift in the shark infested water, wondering if I would first be consumed by my own self loathing or drown in the viscous ocean of alcohol.

Despite my intimate experience with it, the ugly reality of war was never clear to me until this time. I frequently woke in the middle of the night, not with the images of the men whom I had killed but rather with the images of my close friends who were still in harm's way being hurt or worse. Entering a crowded room was not even an option, especially if alcohol was involved. If a stranger brushed against my back in a bar my entire body would tense up and I would immediately go into a sort of primal defensive mode. I would scan the room for threats while moving with haste to a corner where I could more easily defend myself. As a result, I would avoid crowded establishments in favor of the dank dark dive bars in the west valley of Phoenix. Without thinking about it, I would frequently scan rooftops for snipers and was constantly in a hyper vigilant state.

While all of this was going on, I had been in the testing process for the Peoria Fire Department. It was a position that I had coveted since I was a young child. I spent a great deal of time in the stations when I was a boy since my parents were divorced and my father had custody of my sisters and I. I grew to respect the job that those men did everyday with the highest authority. At nineteen, I was fortunate enough to be hired on to a smaller department, a job that I would eventually leave to join the military. As a teenager, I imagined what it would be like to wear the same uniform as my father and possibly, one day, be on the scene of a fire with him.

If there was one place that respected what I had gone through during my time in service it was with the members of that department. The way that my resume was worded would not be off putting to the members of the interview board that sat adjacent to me. In all, the testing process took several months. I had successfully navigated the written test, the physical agility test, and the first interview. I was asked back for the final interview. During the course of this process I had lost one brother in Iraq and seen several others injured. I had seen my resume rejected by just about every organization that I handed it to. My feelings of self-worth were at an all-time low and the guilt of leaving my brothers had become insurmountable.

The day before my final interview, I sat down to lunch with my father and a close family friend, Billy Morris, and explained to them that I could not in good conscience go through with the hiring process. I had to return to service; my friends were still dying. To this day, it may still have been one of the most difficult things for me to tell my father. I could see his eyes lose a shade of color as I uttered those words. Despite his clear aversion to the idea, he made no real attempt at stopping me. I knew that no one declines a final interview with the fire department and doing so would clearly result in a sort of social black eye for my father. It is something that still troubles me to this day. However, the thought of having a skill set that so few in the world possess and sitting on it while good men were dying was too much for me to bear.

I pulled out my class A uniform, made sure that my medals were in order, and that my reflection could easily be seen in the shine on my boots. I walked into that interview and quickly explained that I was honored to have made it this far, but there was still work to be done. There was a clear look of confusion on their faces as though they had just watched someone commit suicide and didn't know what to do. It was a unique, gut-wrenching relief that I would be able to get back in the fight.

Chapter 4: Future Wars

My plan was to enter the Air Force. I would go through selection for a little known Special Operations unit called Pararescue. Known as PJs by those who have had the fortune of working with them, Pararescuemen are the best combat search and rescue men in the US military. Their mission is not direct action in nature. Their primary purpose is to come to the aid of military members in need. Everyone was a trained paramedic, a course that I had already completed, as well as military free-fall, jump and scuba qualified. I had already passed a number of the required courses in their particular pipeline already as well as had a great deal of experience in combat search and rescue. Among other missions, I had spent several days in the Konar Province of Afghanistan in search of the four US Navy SEALs that were compromised on Operation Red Wings.

I couldn't think of a more perfect position. The main role of Pararescue is to come to the aid of those in need. It was a position that I needed to be in, for me and for them. There was only one small problem. Despite my extensive schooling and experience, the Air Force would not talk to me because of a tattoo on my leg. The policy in place was that no more than 25% of any exposed limb while in uniform should be covered by a tattoo. Since the Air Force considered PT shorts and t-shirt a uniform, I was not eligible for service. The tattoo in question is in no way vulgar, it is a painting done by Michael Giordano of the archangel but it covers my entire lower leg. I tried without luck to get a waiver from the Air Force. When that didn't work, I went to my network.

I knew one former PJ in the area named Bob. Bob was a recruit when my father was a training officer in the fire academy. I met him when I was 17 years old when I began testing for the local fire departments. When I made the decision to enlist, he guided me toward being a Ranger. I paid him a visit at his station and asked if he knew anyone who could pull any strings. Bob put me in contact with the Non Commissioned Officer in Charge (NCOIC) of a Pararesuce team about 100 miles away in Tucson. He informed me that they would be holding an in-house trial and that if I could pass then they could easily get me into the unit.

I took to training immediately. I knew that proficiency in the water was going to be a big hurdle so I took to the pool every day. I worked on everything that Bob suggested. I practiced crossover drills and buddy breathing techniques. I trained to be able to swim

75 meters underwater while fatigued. I got my 3 mile run time under 17 minutes and learned everything about PJ history that I could. I stopped drinking entirely, so much so that I offered to be the designated driver on Saint Patrick's Day. For the first time in nearly five months, I had a purpose.

Recently I heard someone say that there are three words that cure PTSD, "You are hired." I believe that it goes beyond that; I believe that a true sense of purpose can help mitigate the toll certain stresses take on us. A true purpose in life is more potent than any medication. When I arrived for that selection I was ready. I had made a half-dozen folders with every military accolade that I had received as well as my updated resume. On the cover of the folder was the Pararescue crest with their motto, "That others may live." I knew that at the end of the selection there would be an interview board and I was prepared to show them that I was not only physically capable but a strong candidate because of my attention to detail and desire to be a member of their team.

I was surprised to see about twenty people arrive for the selection, one of which was another former Ranger medic named Eric. I knew of him but never actually met him before this. He had the exact same issue that I had, and ironically enough, he had his entire arm covered in a very similar archangel tattoo. It didn't take long for us to buddy up. We started the day with a PT test. We did push-ups, sit-ups, pull-ups, a three-mile run and a one-mile swim test. The candidates who didn't pass were informed that they could continue on but likely wouldn't be selected. I wasn't one of those people. I ran a 16:54 three mile on a track and did equally as well on the other events. The real fun, however, began after the PT test was over. We were tortured in the pool for several hours, sprayed with the hose while doing flutter kicks and being screamed at. It was honestly the best time I had in a very long time. I was instantly reminded of the torture that we endured during Ranger Indoctrination and felt very much at ease with my place in the world.

Within a few hours Eric and I began to test the instructor's desire to make us suffer. When doing four count exercises we would sound off with, "can't-smoke- a-rock" instead of the standard, "one-two-three" cadence. To our absolute surprise, the instructors admired our positive attitude. It was totally different from being a Ranger. "Suffer in silence" was a kind of unofficial motto during our selection process so displays of motivation were met with harsher beatings. Anything they threw at us, we ate it up: ruck marches with soaking wet feet, sprints, crawling through mud puddles, and buddy carries. It was truly invigorating to be doing these things again.

While carrying one of the instructors, we realized that we had been on a mission together in Afghanistan two years earlier. When I set him down in front of the training building, the senior instructor said that I would have a spot if I could choke out the instructor that I had just been carrying. As my hands snapped immediately into a fighting position, the lead instructor shouted, "Joking, joking…"

The men in the PJ unit just shook their heads in unison as one of them said, "Fucking Rangers."

I was the first one back from the buddy run and was told to go wait inside. The members that the team wanted to interview were allowed inside while the others were told that they would be calling them later. We were able to take a shower and change for our interview. I gave each member of the board the packets that I had prepared prior to my interview. When I came in and sat down they appeared very angry with me. One of them held up his copy and proclaimed, "What the fuck is this?"

"The Pararescue patch." I replied

"Yeah, no shit, asshole! But why is the corner of the wing cut off? Do you not think that we take this seriously? They don't teach attention to detail in the Rangers?"

I was so confused. I had them printed up at Kinkos and one of them must have printed with a tiny part of one of the wings missing.

"No excuse, Sergeant." Was my only reply. I wasn't going to try to make an excuse; I had fucked up. I didn't apologize. I just repeated that there was no excuse for my mistake.

"Dude... we're fucking with you! You did a spectacular job executing every task during this selection, but this packet just puts it over the top. We want you on our team."

I couldn't believe it. Just like that. I understood fully that I had not even begun the journey, but I had a path. I had a purpose. The interview was supposed to be twenty minutes long but was over in about 60 seconds. I think they just wanted to see if I would talk my way out of my mistake. I was told that since the other recruits were out in the hallway that I couldn't go out just yet. For the next fifteen minutes, to fill the time, we sat and told stories about different missions that we had been on and other guys that we mutually knew. I walked out of that room ten feet tall. Nothing was guaranteed but I was at least going to be given a shot at being a PJ, or so I thought.

The desire to return to military service is common for many veterans. The overwhelming visceral drive to remove oneself from such an environment returns three fold as a need to return in some ironic twist of perception. I do not know a single veteran personally who has not, at some point, spoke of returning to service. The external reasons listed may all be different but internally it comes down to three things, the guilt associated with leaving before the job was done, the longing for the security of all that the military provides, and a general inability to relate to civilians. There is a feeling of being a foreigner in your own country. Basic adult interactions can create an atmosphere of anxiety.

I was finding my place once again among my old group of friends; however, many of them had at least some sense of what I had been doing for the past four years.

Chapter 5: He is Here, He is Not Afraid

"That's my seat that you're sitting in."

"I didn't see your name on it." Replied the 5'2", 100 pound, twenty-something as she shot me a cocky smile. Her arms and chest were covered in tattoos and her jet-black hair hung just above shoulder length.

"Let me rephrase that. If you don't get the fuck out of my chair I'm going to kick you out of it!" Despite the poorly lit, dank bar atmosphere, it was easy to see her eyes fixate on me. It was as if she had never had someone speak to her in such a way. I thought for a moment that my liquor was speaking for me again when she stormed off in an appalled state, but I had only had a couple of whiskeys so that couldn't have been it. My good friend Mike B. struck me on the shoulder as I reclaimed the seat that I had just left to refill my cocktail.

"What the fuck, Leo?" he laughed, "Why would you say that to her?"

"What are you talking about, Mike?"

"You just threatened to kick that girl, who was obviously flirting with you, in the face!"

"I never said where I would kick her, just that I would."

"Dude, she sat in your seat because she likes you."

"What? Why didn't she just say so?"

Mike just shook his head, mumbling something about me being crazy as we joked about my "Lack of game." However, it extended far beyond that. My lexicon had shifted over the past few years. The way that I viewed things was different.

Family relationships were not the only ones that I failed to grow during my time in service. It wasn't evident at the time but being all but completely removed from the opposite sex for years was clearly detrimental to my ability to pick up a girl at a bar. The reality of being a Ranger is that you are isolated from females for extended periods of time and the conversations that predominate your dialogue are constructed in grunts and 'fuck you's'. This is not to say that the men of the 75th are unintelligent, it's just that the way in which we chose to communicate with one another typically consisted of threats of physical violence. We lived a particularly violent lifestyle for good reason. I fully understand that a large portion of our society looks at violence with disdain. There is a belief that only the lower man would stoop to such a resolution in favor of talking through a conflict.

Let me assure you there is no human in our society that dislikes war more than the soldier who has to fight in it, has to bear its burden and hide the scars associated with it from those without the testicular fortitude to make themselves filthy with it. We hide our scars so that you don't have to face the discomfort associated with having to hear the stories of how we got them.

Those scars were earned in the midst of a level of violence that most people don't have the totality to comprehend. We have those scars, they exist, they are real. We have scars instead of a chunk of granite because our commitment to violence surpassed those who wished to do us harm. When violence is the only thing that keeps you and your brothers alive, I assure you that you will adopt it as a way of life. If you deny that statement, you are one of three things: a liar, a fool, or a dead man.

In this we are not ashamed of our violent tendencies and do not feel an overwhelming desire to change them. They have served us well and kept us alive. While we realize that adopting a gentler tone will serve our purpose more effectively the transition is not simple. Solve et coagula involves more than the flip of a switch. In order to adopt a new colloquial lexicon, we must first dissolve the one to which we have become accustomed. We see this often with the shifting of regional dialect or strong accent when a person moves to a new place. Think about how you speak as a woman when there are only women present or as a man when only other men are present. Now think about that conversation occurring without the interruption of the opposite sex for several years. Those speech patterns and mannerisms will undoubtedly be significantly affected. To this day, I still catch myself slipping back into my "old accent" as a stream of unintentional aggressive obscenities fall from my tongue.

Those patterns extend beyond conversation. I once had a girl tell me after sex, "When I'm with you I feel like a pirate." I'm not sure if it was because I have a lot of tattoos or because the sexual aggression which dripped from every pore. Like the late nights I spent in bars or the death sentence workouts I would conduct in the gym, my sexual experiences were an extension of the blitzkrieg behavior that was encouraged in Ranger battalion. When you believe with every beat of your heart that you are not going to live to see 30, there is a tendency to live recklessly. Consequences are no longer problematic when you don't believe that you will live long enough for them to catch up to you. In the bar or the bedroom, there really were no limits; there was no such thing as going too far.

What I thought of as completely acceptable behavior or conversation was over the top for most people. As a result, I spent more and more time with other self-destructive individuals. It was uncomfortable being around the church goers, the early risers, and the straight arrows. The more time I spent around them: the more of an outcast I felt like.

Waiting for my slot to open for Pararescue Indoc. I began spending more and more time in the dive bars of the west valley. I joined the ranks of a new type of formation. Shoulder to shoulder, dress right dress upon a barstool. To my right, veterans from Vietnam silently drowning their demons with another stale light and domestic. Staring blankly, silently, at the wall of medicine we shared something. We were like medics handling suicide by cyanide with bleeding fingers.

Here I felt at home, where my vernacular would not alienate me. Outside of that dank den of security, the world was judging me for something that they didn't even understand. Here it was safe.

What I thought was a breakthrough in my employment dilemma became another slap in my face. Due entirely to one of my best friends from Ranger Battalion's mothers, I managed to secure a marketing job for a major US brand. I didn't have any experience in marketing, but I was able to learn the ins and outs very quickly. I enjoyed the job very much. It enabled me to get out and interact with various people and required that I used ingenuity to accomplish my objectives.

The wars in Iraq and Afghanistan were still in full swing, a fact that my direct supervisor frequently expressed animus about. She had recently finished graduate school and held vehement opinions about the wars we were fighting. Knowing that I was a veteran, she used every opportunity that she could to berate me about the politics of war. To be honest, I didn't really care. When I enlisted I didn't care about the politics, I didn't care if there was a legal declaration or the long-term consequences. All I cared about was that my country was attacked on my birthday and 343 fellow fire fighters were killed along with thousands of my fellow Americans. During my enlistment, I was a little too busy fighting those wars to study the politics of them. I felt like being there provided me a unique vantage point.

It didn't take long for me to get fed up with her attitude. Responding to her I would frequently say things like, "Yeah, that's not how we did it in Iraq." Or, "bet they don't teach you that in college." It wasn't out of defiance... okay maybe it was a little. One afternoon, we were delivering product to one of the companies sponsored athletes. He was a famous NFL quarterback living in Chandler, Arizona for the off season.

When we arrived at his home late one Saturday morning, he was just brushing off the effects of a hangover, which made two of us. His home was nice but not flashy like I had imagined. As we were unloading the product into his house, he asked if we were hungry at all. My boss looked at me in terror as she said, "No, no, we're good."

"Actually, I am a pretty hungry. Whatcha got?"

In his Barry White like voice he responded, "I got some chicken left ova from a Bah-Bee Que" If you know me at all, you know I'm not going to pass up the opportunity to take some leftovers out of the fridge of a 1st round draft pick. No chance. It was delicious too.

We were supposed to get him to sign a few footballs for future giveaways. As he signed them I couldn't resist, I couldn't pass up the opportunity to catch a pass from a Super Bowl quarterback. I ran a slant route in his front yard and put my hands out. He delivered like Dominos. Right on the numbers.

The drive back to the warehouse was a little tense. Personally, I had a great time and the chicken all but cured my hangover. My boss, on the other hand, was not as titillated as I was.

"I can't believe you would do that, Leo."

"Do what?"

"This isn't a game you know! He could get upset!"

"About what?"

"You raided his fridge then had him play catch with you!"

"And…"

"That's not how things are done!"

"Well, when I was in Iraq…"

Suffice it to say, I didn't work there much longer. No matter, I would be in the Air Force soon enough and wouldn't have to worry about offending people so easily.

Chapter 6: Harder Harmonies

It had been three months since I had successfully passed the in-house selection for the Pararescue team in Tucson. In that time I was fortunate enough to be visited by a few of my very close friends from Ranger Battalion, including my former roommates Morty and Jess. I couldn't help but miss the strong sense of belonging and purpose that once flooded my veins. The three-day visits were invigorating for my soul and I couldn't wait for my opportunity to rejoin another Special Operations unit. I called the person in charge of the team on a regular basis in an attempt to figure out when I would be allowed to go to Indoc -- the ten week selection process that would grant access to the rest of the PJ pipeline. After months of inquiries, I was informed that there was little chance that the waiver would go through and my tattoos were going to end up keeping me out of service after all.

My academy date for the fire department had already come and gone. I had placed all of my eggs in a single basket and that basket just slipped from my fingers. Within an hour of receiving the notice that I would not be joining the Air Force, I received a phone call from a very close friend from another former Ranger roommate who was living in Chicago. We had served together as medics in the 75th before I went to 3rd Ranger battalion. Matt got out of the Army a couple of months before I did and had been making use of his business degree working as a consultant. He would frequently call and tell me how much he disliked his new role and the people he worked with. He had decided to move back to Indiana and take the prerequisite classes necessary to get into medical school. I took a few minutes to get him caught up on my situation. Without hesitation Matt asked, "Why don't you just move to Indiana and go to school with me?" Silence fell over our conversation. "I'll call you back," and I hung up the phone.

I pulled the frosty half full bottle of Jameson from my freezer and poured a double. I looked at my fat lazy little brown dog and asked what she thought about moving to the Midwest as I shot the libation. I dispensed another tall pour into my glass and continued the conversation with the mutt. "It is cold there, buddy. You've never seen snow before. What do you think?"

Since she did little more than wag her tail, I assumed she was okay with the decision. I walked into my room, pulled my large duffle bag from my closet and called Matt. As the phone rang I began tossing my possessions into the bag.

"What's up dude?" Answered Matt.

"I'll be there in three days."

There really wasn't anything left for me in the town I grew up in. Moving on feels so right when nothing else does. It's like the city's got it's own song but I couldn't play along. I saw the notes as they flew by but always played them wrong. Now a fresh start, a new chance to find the harmony.

Despite being the most mind numbing drive of my entire life, I was invigorated at the notion of being reunited with such a close friend, a person that had been experiencing the same hardships that I had since leaving service. This reunion would be one of the most impactful of my post-military experience.

I'm not entirely sure if places like Ranger Battalion attract a certain type of personality or create it. What I am sure of is that being in such close proximity to so many like-minded individuals is something that I feel most take for granted. Following years of a very unique form of suppression, it is natural to rebel and remove yourself from important aspects of that life. In doing so, it is common to disconnect from the only other personalities that are like your own. Along with reinstatement of purpose, the reconnection with individuals that are familiar with your plight without having to speak a word has the greatest positive impact on a veteran's ability to be effective in society. At some point, post-military, these men go from being Ranger buddies to Ranger brothers; behind the brown fence, a person that you may give little more than a passing nod to would instantly become your best of friends during a random encounter years later.

The drive from Phoenix to South Bend Indiana consisted of about a thousand miles of cornfields. It was nearly maddening. Just corn, more corn, and then a little more corn. I never wanted to see corn ever again when I got out of that truck. Being welcomed by Matt's family with a full-on turkey dinner complete with corn on the cob was almost a cruel joke. The way that you cannot turn down your own mother's home cooking, I could not decline an extra helping. Matt's family had taken me in as a sixth son during my time in the military. I had gotten to know them well through various graduation ceremonies, family celebrations and trips home. This included the infamous trip to Notre Dame following my second deployment, which resulted in one of their sons and I being banned from campus for life.

Matt was still tying up a few loose ends in Chicago and was a little surprised when I got to Indiana before he did. It would be several days before he would arrive in South Bend. I used that time to look for a place for the two of us to live. I found a perfect house directly across from the campus that Matt and I would be attending. In the three days spanning from the time I received the invite from Matt and the time I stepped off to embark on my trip across the Midwest, I applied to the Indiana University satellite campus in South Bend. Prior to joining the military, I chose to graduate high school early so I attended classes at a local college until being hired by a fire department. I had maintained a 3.9 grade point average during those three semesters that I was in community college, a fact that no doubt helped gain admittance into the University.

The adventurous act of moving halfway across the country to live with a Ranger buddy in order to attend a school that I had never seen, with people whom I had never met, was exhilarating. Being with a friend that knew me as well as any other human alive was therapeutic. It was like the good old days when we lived together in a tiny dungeon-like barracks room in Ft. Benning, Georgia. Uttering a simple sentence that none of my good friends in Phoenix could understand, would send Matt into an obnoxious fit of laughter. Honestly, he is quite possibly one of the most pompous, crude, vulgar, disgusting, amazing human beings I have ever encountered. His crooked smile and infrequently revolving wardrobe made joking about his lawful inability to get close to an elementary school very easy. The man could drink his weight in alcohol, but after the second drink he would be magically transformed from intellect to halfwit. In short, he was a lot like me, completely rough around the edges but would give you the shirt off of his back in an instant.

Exercise physiology had been my previous course of study, however, that was not an offered major so I was undecided my first semester. I decided to take a political science class focusing on international relations, along with a class in Sociology, English and Public Speaking. During my first week, I had some difficulty focusing on the lectures. I would look around at the young faces and couldn't help but feel out of place. The temperate, air conditioned environment was a stark contrast to my previous learning environment. I began to feel guilty. I began to feel a strong sense of cognitive dissonance. It wasn't that long ago that I sat in a tent in Iraq mocking the soft, incapable college students that lived for nothing but their own self-serving tendencies. Now I found myself among them. I was one of them and for some reason I resented myself for it.

For the most part, I kept my service quiet. During one discussion in my political science course the subject of Iraq came up. I sat witness to more false statements in that conversation than stocks of corn on my drive through Illinois. The role of private contracting companies like Blackwater and their part in the war took over the conversation. Statements as bold as "treasonous murderers," and "baby killing opportunists" spewed from the mouths of the uniformed children. Some of my best friends were now employed by that organization. Following the tenth flippant comment, I could no longer restrain myself. I asked bluntly if anyone in the room had ever been to Iraq or if they had any actual experience with the organizations that they found so easy to belittle. Of the close to fifty students, not one could say that they had any firsthand experience with the subject matter in which they were so fervently professing.

Following my inquiry, I informed the class that I had spent time in Iraq and that I know several of the people who were being demonized in their conversation. The statement that rang out from a student in the back row still makes my eye tick.

"The real terrorists aren't the ones in caves, the real terrorists are the ones who volunteered to fight in Bush's war."

It took a brief moment to process what he said. Until this point, I had not experienced such a blatant

disrespect for my service. I was just called a terrorist...
by an American citizen. I wanted to pick up my desk
and throw it at his face. I was overcome with rage. My
right eye ticked and my dominant hand trembled from a
combination of adrenaline and the instant memory of all
the violence that I had bathed in for the sake of those
like him. I attempted to respond verbally but could
muster little more than a slight audible scoff. I rose
from my seat and exited the classroom.

As I stood in that hallway, I thought of my
friends who would never walk the same again and those
buried in Arlington. I wanted to open the gates of hell
and allow the entirety of its wrath to flow upon the
wretched people in that room. A thought slipped into
my head at that moment. I was one of the people in that
room. I was no longer making a change in the world; I
was listening to people banter about other people
making a difference in the world. It was too much for
me to digest. I went directly home and rather than
returning with a .45, I poured a pint of whiskey and
exhumed old habits.

By the time that Matt returned from class, I was
listening to the song *Farewell Soldier* on repeat and had
to squint to make out his face as he entered the door. He
chuckled at my inebriated state. I slurred the words, "I
fucking hate people." He didn't even ask. It's not that
he didn't care, he just knew.

"Yup, you wanna go to the Oaken Bucket and
get a beer?" I didn't need someone to take pity on me. I
needed someone that understood what that transition
felt like. I needed to know that I wasn't alone in the
world. Matt silently shouldered the support I needed
during this time. Having a man like that around did

more for me than any therapist could ever hope to do. My own family, despite their good intentions, could never provide the simple solace of a few beers with a friend like that; a person that knew what it was like.

I had a friend, now I really needed a job. It had been close to a year since I had anything that resembled a real employment and despite being a full time student, my feeling of self-worth was still very low. In my sociology class, I found myself frequently disagreeing with the subject matter. Concepts like the caste system seemed highly absurd to me. The idea that a person cannot rise above the position of their birth was in direct conflict to the American ideals that my friends and I fought for. Furthermore, I had several very good friends that had never stepped foot in a college classroom that were making well into the six figures at 23 years old. They were capitalizing on their skill sets. That is what makes our nation great, the ability to improve based on your willingness to work hard and create opportunity.

It was impossible for me to sit by as thirty-six impressionable young minds mindlessly took notes on this professor's idea of how our society works. I found myself researching every topic prior to the meeting of our class so that I could intelligently combat the foolish things that she uttered. Each week I would take the fight to the enemy in her own arena. During one lecture, she made the statement that if every American had the chance to be president for two weeks then we would see positive change. I couldn't help but laugh out loud as soon as she said this. She was used to me laughing at her ideas by this point. I suggested that we implement her idea right now, in her class. Perhaps if you allowed each student to teach a class throughout the semester then we would see a positive change. To this day I'm not sure if she hated me or loved the fact that one of her students paid such close attention.

Beyond improving my debate skills, that class was where I met a fellow student named Patrick Kulwicki. Pat was a tall thin guy with dark hair. His attire frequently suggested that he was a cyclist. The class was held just once a week for a couple of hours long. We were given a short break in the middle of class to stretch our legs and use the restroom. During one of these intermissions, I struck up a conversation with Pat. We had several things in common including cycling. He informed me that he worked at a local outdoor store called Outpost Sports. He worked on bikes in the summer and skis in the winter. He informed me that they were getting ready to hire. This seemed like a really cool job.

When I got home, I told Matt about the job. He replied, "Oh yeah, Outpost. That's JV's place. My parents have known that guy forever." The knowledge that my surrogate family was close friends with the owner gave me hope that it wouldn't be another dry hole. I completely bullshitted my way through the interview. "Yeah I've done a lot of hiking." In Afghanistan..."Oh yeah, I love snowboarding." I loved it the one time that I went…

I needed this job and not just for the money. So many potential employers had turned me away over the past year that the thought of adding one more to the list was more than I could bear.

To my surprise, I got the job. I was told that I would be selling snowboards for the most part, a thing I knew nothing about. That didn't bother me in the slightest. It's been said that the only thing a member of US Special Operations needs is an Internet connection and twelve hours and they will be an expert on anything that they need to be. I grabbed every snowboard review guide and manufacturer catalog put out over the past three seasons. By the start of my first day, I was able to talk shop about cambered versus rockered and effective edge to length ratios. This stick has the pop if you're looking to hit the jibs. You want that all mountain ride though if you're going out west.

As with any demographic, it is not accurate to say that all veterans make perfect candidates for any position that they may apply for, but I can confidently speak for the majority of the men and women that have lived and worked in a combat environment in saying that adapting to a task is not a skill, it is a way of life. We have gained an intimate understanding of what we are capable of, having volunteered to place ourselves in the most trying environments imaginable. We know that any hurdle, be it physical or mental, is easily navigated given the proper motivation. Our shoulders are broad from bearing the burden of so many for so long. We are resourceful in times of scarcity and steadfast in the face of vicissitude.

The notion of hiring a person who has little to no experience in the industry where they are applying is no doubt unnerving for someone responsible for selecting the most qualified candidate. Add to this the often over inflated sense of self-worth that many veterans carry and the task becomes nearly insurmountable. Being a veteran carries with it a nearly palpable sense of pride for most who have served. This is a characteristic that many wear on their sleeves. That pride, while being a sought-after attribute in the military, is viewed as a boastful arrogance to many civilians. Having a three-page resume highlighting actions on combat missions exemplifies this type of attitude. In 2007, it was my personal belief that I shouldn't have to tone down my experiences in order to fit in or get a job. Support your troops magnets were affixed to a seemingly endless row of bumpers, echoing the sentiment that our society is here to prop up those who have willing given their best years in support of the greater good.

I understand that many people will take offence to the following statement, but it has been my experience, along with almost every other veteran that I have spoken with, that that type of support is little more than lip service from the majority of those who tout it. It is easy to say thank you to a young soldier at the gas station or pay for his fill up because it gives you a particularly good and patriotic feeling. It is a completely other thing to put some of your own skin in the game and hire that person for a job that they have little experience. That is real support. That carries a resonating impact on their future and exemplifies that what they have done has not gone without notice.

Chapter 7: The Castle builders

College was an interesting experience for me, as a 25 year old combat veteran. Where many other students were enamored by the very presence of certain teachers, I tended to be unimpressed. It was difficult to admire a person who stood in front of a group of malleable young minds and preached an ethos on worldly topics when I knew that they have never left the state in which they currently reside. By the midterm of my first semester, I found myself arguing with my teachers more and more. This defiance was not necessarily new from an internal sense, however, there was no outlet for it in the military. Even if you disagreed with an instructor or superior officer there was seldom a way of expressing that without bringing about catastrophe.

This is an important designation for any professors currently reading this. When you look out upon the sea of new faces on the first day of class and gaze upon that one steely eyed, scruffy student wearing a hat with an American flag and who is a little older than the rest of the group, it is crucial that you understand something: This person has had almost every opinion of theirs suppressed for years. Your classroom is a candy shop for a kid that has been on a forced diet. As soon as that person realizes that they are authorized to disagree, they will let worries wander out like water streaming from a spring. It is also important for you not to assume that since they chose a path of violence that they are incapable of intellectual debate. This particular student is highly accustomed to being engaged in conflict and holds egregious the notion of giving up ground.

Personally, I kept a notebook in class for such things. Not in the way that most students kept a notebook, for the sake of preparing for some arbitrary test or final. My notebook was for marking the inaccuracies of everything that the subject matter expert in front of us claimed to be true. Upon returning home, countless hours would be spent researching, again not the subject matter for a test, but rather for the accuracy of the statements made by the teacher. These would be points that would be brought up with force during the next class. In the military, accurate information and attention to detail are paramount. The bullshit meter typically doesn't go as high with this type of student.

When discussing the need for increased awareness of the feminist movement, one of my teachers made the mistake of stating that women have a greater capacity for endurance than men. When I inquired as to what she meant by this she stumbled through an absurd explanation. A statement along the lines of, "If a man and a women both started running at the same time the man would die before the woman would." She then attempted to move on beyond the moronic statement but I wasn't having that. It was like a cage fighter who sees that their opponent just slipped and fell and I had every intention on capitalizing on her statement.

I hijacked the next thirty minutes of class to explain to her, from a physiological, scientifically-supported perspective, that she was all fucked up. She had made similar statements in previous classes and I could stand it no more. I explained to her the dangers of misleading impressionable young minds with false information. This is a stand that I have come to take on many things these days. Truth is obviously an important thing, but when a group of people pays an outrageous amount of money to learn from a person who is supposed to be smarter than they are, then there is a moral and social obligation to speak the truth, always. The smallest pebble of misinformation will undoubtedly create such a massive ripple when tossed into the minds of the youth, that its impact will reach the furthest shore.

I felt an obligation to question the information being dispensed by those in power. The structure of a classroom is set up so much like that of a dictatorship that not speaking out could quickly lead to a draconian rule. As misguided as it may have been, the teachers and other students in those classrooms became the enemy. The more I questioned the autonomy of the instructor, the more I was looked at with disdain. This simply fueled my fire. Comments from teachers on papers that I had written stating, "This sentence doesn't make sense" resulted in a response of, "Maybe you're just not smart enough to understand it."

Now even if it was true, saying so is a sure-fire way of creating a tumultuous environment. People that have spent the majority of their life in a classroom do not take kindly to some dumb soldier insinuating that they have a higher degree of intellect than they do. Perhaps it's pride or disbelief but in the seventy college courses that I have completed, I can count on one hand the number of teachers that acknowledged my experience as a valuable contribution to the class. More than once, I had to take my argument to a department head because I received a subpar grade on a paper. More often than not, it was because I took the furthest extreme in opinion from my teacher and suffered the lashings of the red pen as a result.

After three semesters at the satellite campus of Indiana University, I had decided that I needed a bigger pond to swim in. There were a few good teachers at the smaller school, but I longed for the real college experience. I wanted to be on the big campus that I had seen in so many movies. I wanted the total college experience.

I ended up at Purdue through an interesting circumstance. I knew that I wasn't long for IUSB. I asked my roommate Matt if Purdue was actually in Indiana. Of course, he responded in the way that he typically did, "Jenkins, you're an idiot." This either meant that it very much was or very much was not in our state, so I resorted to an Internet search. I had been, as per the norm, pretty drunk. By the time I found the University's website, I was nearly in a blacked-out state. Two weeks later, Matt entered our home with a large envelope with my name printed on the front. "Did you apply to Purdue?" He asked with a surprised inflection.

"I don't think so…. Maybe. I don't know."

The cover letter enclosed stated something stated something along the lines of:

Mr. Jenkins,
Upon receiving your essay and application for entry to Purdue University we are pleased to…. et cetera, et cetera.

I told Matt, "I guess I got drunk and applied to college again." He just shook his head. Nothing I ever did really surprised him. The fact is that we have been such good friends for so long because we may be the only two people on this earth that will readily dismiss the ridiculous actions of the other. To this day, I still don't recall writing that essay.

Chapter 8: Stay Happy There

By this point in my life, moving to an unknown place had become second nature. I had uprooted and started over so many times during my childhood, during my time in the military, and now in my post-service travels that I found a slight discomfort in staying in any place too long.

Familiarity became a noose. I only knew one person at Purdue. We worked together from time to time at the snowboard shop and he was also transferring from IUSB. Since neither of us knew anyone else near campus it seemed fitting to find a place together. Our first option was a large group house that we would go in on with a few other guys. Ultimately that fell through so we began looking at two and three bedroom places.

When viewing a place a mile or so off of campus, my acquaintance asked me a question that I was not prepared for. "So you're not gonna kill me in my sleep cause of your PTSD from Iraq, right?"

Whether it was a joke or serious concern, it was unsettling either way. I couldn't believe it. I was accustomed to people misunderstanding my position on certain issues and even being overly delicate with me in regards to certain subject matter, but this guy just came right out and delivered as flippant a remark as I've heard to date. *Was this how other people felt around me? Is this how the population viewed its returning warriors? Are we some sort of extreme liability that they'll be forced to tiptoe around in hopes of not arousing provocation?* I couldn't live with this person. Hell, I didn't want to be in the same room with him after that.

I ended up renting a small apartment above an old house just off campus alone; a place that I was hoping would be a base camp for a series of new adventures. Immediately after I moved in, there seemed to be a buzz regarding the old guy that was moving in upstairs. The other four occupants of the house were all starting their sophomore year and were a shade light of their 21st birthday. They helped me unload the two truckloads of possessions that I had acquired since departing from Phoenix. We shared a drink in the backyard as we became acquainted and quickly addressed what I am sure was the burning question on each of their minds. "Just let me know if you guys want me to pick up any booze for you whenever."

"Ohhh yeah, I mean, that's cool, if you want to. No worries though." They collectively replied with a tone of excitement and relief. I had been in West Lafayette for 15 minutes and I had already made three friends. In fact I still speak with one of them, Nick, to this very day.

It didn't take long to figure out that regardless of the size of campus or number of programs offered, the attitude of most students and teachers was about the same as my previous experience. On the first day of class, I sat eagerly in the front row. Admittedly, the reason for this was after multiple combat deployments in Afghanistan and Iraq, my hearing was terrible and there was no way I was going to be able to hear the lecture if I sat in the back of this sixty student classroom. However, my plan was to lay low and not spotlight myself. I was here to blend in with and finally become a student.

Purdue was the real deal, a Big Ten school that is nationally ranked for its academics. The instructor started his lecture by letting us know that we would be discussing several topics that people may hold strong opinions about, yet regardless of the subject matter that we should remain calm and dignified in our speech toward one another. He added that there is no need to bring emotion into a political debate. Within the first ten minutes of the first lecture he began discussing Iraq. My degree focus was International Relations and Iraq was very much a focal point in foreign policy at the time, so it made sense to open the class with this. In an effort to remain neutral, I avoided engaging the man when he referred to the conflict as "Bush's war." When the statement was made that the president should be impeached for illegally going to war I could no longer hold it in.

"We're not at war, sir."

"Excuse me? What's your name?"

"It's Leo, sir. And you are incorrect. President Bush never declared war. Technically we are engaged in multiple, long-term operations. Hence, Operation Enduring Freedom and Operation Iraqi Freedom."

"Well, Leo... you tell the men with their boots in that dirt that there isn't a war going on and see how they respond."

I thought this a strong emotional based attack coming from the same gentlemen who moments before urged us to leave such tactics out of our debates. So I made it all of 15 minutes into the first class of my first day of my first semester at Purdue before I showed my hand. "Well sir, I've been to both Iraq and Afghanistan as a member of US Special Operations. My boots have been covered in that dirt you speak of. They have been stained with the mud and blood and brains from fighting in each nation. I can tell you firsthand that we, the people who carry the burden, don't give a rat's ass what it's called and we sure as shit stand behind our Commander in Chief."

In the military we call this an "escalation of force." I wasn't about to play his game, not now or ever. The type of man that insists that I call him Doctor is the kind of man that I insist calls me Sergeant. I earned that title as he earned his. I, for one, am not one to capitulate to a fancy piece of paper on a man's wall. His accolades did little to impress me. He lost my attention and respect within minutes of taking my seat.

Class after class I ran into the same issues. A person who has spent the majority of their life in an air-conditioned classroom preaching about how the world works to a group of impressionable minds on autopilot.

Most of the information being taught was not particularly accurate in regards to the Middle East and taught with such a spin that it was borderline infuriating. The worst part was that no one was questioning it. Furthermore, I was ostracized when I did. My peers used to be the most elite fighting force of our generation. Now I was sitting beside those who had no concept of what their freedom of speech had cost. Two years since I had left the brown fence and the only thing that had changed was the length of my facial hair and the number of tattoos etched on my skin.

It was a very uncomfortable time. I attempted to escape the discomfort of my dissociation by increasing my training volume. A common day consisted of waking up at five in the morning and heading to the pool to swim three to four miles. I would show up to my 8AM class smelling like chlorine with goggle marks prominently surrounding my eyes. After my morning class, I would often ride my bicycle to Illinois. It was about a hundred and twenty miles round trip. I would attend my afternoon class then head to the gym for at least an hour of CrossFit or lifting. I would finish my day with a half a bottle of booze. While traditionally I have always been a Jameson guy, I was on a pretty big rum kick during those days. There is nothing wrong with living a healthy lifestyle and incorporating fitness into your daily routine, but I wasn't living a healthy lifestyle. I wasn't running for health, I was running away from it. I was running away from the ever-growing army of demons in my own mind.

By the end of my first semester I was having doubts about my decision to leave my place with Matt. I cannot emphasize enough the importance of keeping company with those who have walked the same treacherous roads you have. I tried to keep my focus on my end game. Graduate and apply for a position with the DEA. I wanted to work on their FAST team since meeting one on them a couple of years before. As fate would have it, I wouldn't have to wait as long as I initially thought.

I received an email on the last day of November from a medic I used to work with that I will call "Hendrix." He asked if I was interested in a position with the DEA. I responded in jest that that is the reason why I'm sitting through all of these bullshit college classes. He informed me that a position had opened up for a team medic in one of the Foreign-deployed Advisory Support Teams (FAST) in Afghanistan and he had already vetted me. The job was mine if I wanted it, but I would have to act quickly.

He needed an answer NOW. Finals were just two and a half weeks away. Hendrix informed me that they would need me on a plane before that. If I wanted the opportunity, then I would have to respond today. As most of my major life decisions go, I decided that the only logical thing to do would be to pour a stiff glass of whiskey and let it simmer for a moment...moment's over... *I'm in.*

The single ice cube in my glass didn't even have time to melt. This was the very reason why I was sitting through these classes. Why sit through more aggravating lessons if my dream job was calling me now. It all happened very quickly. Hendrix overnighted a packet full of paperwork that needed to be filled out and returned within 48 hours. I asked each of my teachers if I could be allowed to take the final a week and a half early. Each of them gave me a strange look when I told them that I had a business trip out of the country, all of them with the exception of one. He had been a Marine in Vietnam. I usually sat in the front row in his 400-student class. I showed up early and asked questions frequently. Once or twice throughout the semester I wore one of my Ranger PT shirts. When I told him I was leaving the country on business he just said, "Don't say another word. Don't worry about your final. Be safe."

I found myself overcome with a sense of brotherhood in this moment. Regardless that we served in different branches and of our generational gap, they're maintained a sense of solidarity and support. I had respected this man before, but in this moment I felt instantly connected to the fraternity of veterans the world over. This was one of my first experiences with the totality of the veteran network.

The rest of my teachers did not respond as favorably. Most seemed very inconvenienced by the request. Regardless of their disapproval, I breezed through each of my respective final tests and boarded a plane within a week of receiving the call from Hendrix.

Chapter 9: A World of Welcome and Warning

Going back to Afghanistan two years after I got out could provide a multitude of pitfalls for my eventual reintegration into society, but I wasn't thinking about that at the time. The notion of being surrounded by other people like me was too much to pass up. Once more I would be able to feel the comfortable weight of an M5 aid bag, something that I missed dearly. It may sound odd, but something as simple as being called Doc is enough to revive one's self worth.

The Wild West is the only place for a cowboy. The war zone is the only place for a warrior. It is where we feel at home. It is where we know that the people around us are for us. They live for us and would die for us. People in the US speak often of loyalty, friendship and brotherhood. The only place I have ever truly felt those things in my core, in my soul, is in the perfect calmness surrounded by the absolute calamity of unmatched violence that is combat. The moments that define altruism mold a mutual love and understanding that is the sole property of the combat veteran.

My first stop was to the East Coast. It was required before every deployment that your affairs were in order. Physical, dental and eye exams were expedited. It was a small group being sent over, so qualifying in weapons and medical lanes was fairly quick. We had to qualify with a pistol, AK47 and an M4 on a 25m range. Although I hadn't fired a weapon in over two years, I managed a first time go on each of the exercises. We drew uniforms from supply while our Afghan work visas were being issued. The entire process took about four days. A rental car and hotel were provided for the duration, it was an incredibly efficient process.

As I boarded the plane I still didn't know what to expect. I received a quick brief as to how the FAST teams worked, but I certainly didn't have a comprehensive understanding of them. Landing in Dubai for a two-day layover was an incredibly exciting notion to me. I had always wanted to visit as many places in the world as possible, but up until this point, my passport had remained unstamped. Travel to and from countries like Iraq and Afghanistan was conducted in the back of a military cargo plane. This was actually a serious problem for me when returning from my last deployment to Iraq.

I took a civilian flight into London after being injured. I was returning to the United States by myself for surgery. When I attempted to board the flight to

Atlanta they asked for my passport. I simply told them that I don't have one and attempted to board the plane. It came as a bit of a surprise to the gentlemen tearing tickets. He asked me where I was coming from and didn't like it when I told him that I wasn't allowed to say. I wasn't trying to be rude; it was just that Operational Security (OPSEC) had been beaten into me by this point. Had it not been for the two Air Force pilots in line behind me, I would probably still be stuck in England. They explained to the flight attendant the situation and ensured him that my military ID would suffice. I still owe those two a drink.

To be honest, arriving in Dubai was a bit overwhelming. Very few things were in English and everyone was dressed like the people I had spent my early twenties hunting. I felt my right eye tick slightly with anxiety. I moved with the crowd to the customs line. It took everything I had not to look nervous. Here I was, in a country where I didn't speak the language and didn't know a single other human being. It is incredible how absolutely tiny you can feel in a moment like that. I watched with anticipation as the customs officer provided me with my first passport stamp. The first of what would be many in the years to come.

My time in Dubai was short and not very exciting. I'm assuming that the hotel that I stayed in was very nice, but I wasn't able to figure out how to turn on the light switch. One dark hotel room looks like another. After paying twenty dollars for the hamburger at the hotel bar I was happy to be getting back on that plane. The flight into Kabul was short in comparison to the one from the States. I was very fortunate to link up with a couple of US contractors in Dubai who gave me the heads up on what to do when we landed in Afghanistan. Apparently there was a facilitator who would expedite our trip through customs. The cost of $20 seemed well worth the assistance. He slung my 60 lb black duffle bag over his tiny body like a born pack mule and proceeded to take us to the front of the line.

Getting picked up at the airport by an old friend is always a joyous occasion. Being picked up by another former Ranger outside of an airport in a country where there are countless people that would love to cut your head off with a rusty machete is a reunion like no other. Hendrix was a sight for sore eyes. His 'fro had grown significantly since the last time I had seen him and I could tell he had been hitting the weights. A mutual "fuck you" grin is shot across the parking lot as I made my way to his position. Yeah, we bro-hugged. I slid into the backseat of his Toyota 4Runner. Reaching across to the front seat I shook the hand of the man driving. Jim was a former Texas SWAT officer. Unbeknownst to me at the time, Jim and I were to be on the same team and would work closely for the next several months. It was difficult to tell his stature, but he had a strong handshake and a beard so he gained instant credibility with me. Hendrix informed me that there was an AK with three mags and a set of body armor in the back for me.

Hendrix and I had been Ranger medics together in 3rd Ranger Battalion and had done some very cool things, but this was almost too much, this was Operator as Fuck. Just three dudes with beards and AKs dipping through the congestion of Kabul rush hour. No air support, no convoy, no cover of night, just the three of us on our way to God knows where. I was so exhilarated by the notion of it that I didn't even ask what was going on. I didn't care. This was cool. Three cars took up two lanes of traffic as mirrors scraped and bumpers touched. The symphony of horns was actually pleasant. All I had ever known of this nation before today was the silence and vastness of its nights. It was refreshing to know that the capital city was a bustling hive of activity.

We ducked right into a tight alleyway, an act that instantly took me from elated to hyper vigilant. All of my senses turned on automatically and I began scanning the windows and roof tops. After a hundred meters we stopped. Hendrix waved some credentials at an Afghan man with a rifle and he opened the gate behind him. We made the tight turn into a small compound in the middle of Kabul. I was informed that this is where I would be receiving my identification cards. Jim filled the truck with gas while Hendrix helped me fill out a few sheets of paper work and get me up to speed on what is happening in country. Apparently the FAST team was rotated out of the country at the time so operations were pretty slow. After getting four new forms of identification and eating about a dozen of the secretary's cookies, we headed for the truck and made our way across town to the DEA compound.

Before I even unloaded my bag, Hendrix asked if I want to accompany him to a hash run. I had no clue what that was, but I was a big fan of running so I happily agreed. Little did I know that it was more a meeting of great drinkers than great runners. I had no idea that a hash run was an event where people met up to drink and make fun of each other. Hendrix took me to the armory where I drew a pistol and a radio. Shortly after we headed back into town to meet up with a few of his British friends. This became a whole new world for me. The idea of two guys leaving the wire together in Afghanistan for anything was unheard of during our time in Ranger Battalion. Now we just hopped into his truck and went, as if we were in the US. This was beyond a culture shock.

As per the tradition with previous deployments, I was under the impression that it would be several months before I enjoyed a cold beer. Within four hours of landing I had consumed two. It was an early night as I was informed that I would be flying out to a place called Konduz in the morning. For some reason I assumed that Hendrix and I would be working together directly, but apparently my skills were needed elsewhere. In the morning Jim and I boarded King Air, a small private jet that would act as our chariot for the remainder of my time in the country. This was a stark contrast to being crammed in the back of a Chinook helicopter or C130 cargo plane. A guy could get used to this type of treatment.

The wheels of that tiny plane slid as they touched down in the blizzard like conditions of Northern Afghanistan. During my time as a Ranger I had grown to trust the pilots of the 160th Special Operations Aviation Regiment. Their skill was unmatched in the most austere of situations. This pilot matched that skill as he kept the jet from losing control. As we ducked through the tiny door of the aircraft I took note of my surroundings. This wasn't an airport;

this was a flat white strip of land in the middle of nowhere. We might as well have just flown into Siberia. *THIS is where I was going to be spending the next month?*

Two diesel pickups were waiting there to pick up Joe, Jim and myself. Joe was the team RTO (Radio Telephone Operator). He was responsible for all of our communications. I had just met the man but my initial impression was that he was pissed off about something. Possibly being sent to the Arctic Circle had him a little irritated. I would come to learn that Joe was pretty much always pissed off.

After a short ride from the airfield I found myself once again inside the confining grey walls of those HESCO barriers. HESCO barriers are dirt filled wire containers responsible for keeping the bad guys and their projectiles out. They also had the looming side effect of creating a very prison like atmosphere. I instantly felt a sense of claustrophobia set in. My feet stepped over the all too familiar loose stone meant to keep the dust down and it felt like déjà vu. It was like a ghost town there. The compound was nearly a perfect square, not more than a quarter mile in total circumference. Prefabricated white buildings acted as living quarters, chow hall and gym. I was shown to what would be my room for the next 30 days and dropped my single black hockey bag before meeting the rest of the guys for lunch.

The chow hall was no hall at all really. Six or seven mid-sized tables and a short serving line. In that line stood about twenty thin Afghan men in military uniforms. Their sunken weathered faces and dark beards shifted to my direction. I felt 40 hard eyes following me as I made my way to the seat where the other Americans were sitting. There was something comforting and familiar about the moment. It would take well into my second cup of tea before I realized that it was the solace of sitting at a table where every man had a gun on his hip and knew how to use it. There was no swagger in the small group, just an overwhelming confidence that nothing in the world could shake their poise.

I didn't know a single last name among them yet these were the men that I had been missing for the past two years. This was my table and it felt reassuring to sit at it once again. Somehow I had felt out of place sitting among a group of friends from high school when I returned home yet sitting with these nearly perfect strangers was enough to put me at ease.

The next month was filled with amazing new experiences while still feeling incredibly familiar. We spent a great deal of time training the Narcotics Interdiction Unit (NIU). They were a young DEA counterpart but still had relatively little tactical experience and training. Jim and I created mock shoot houses and drilled the men on every possible situation that they may encounter. From breakfast to dinner we went from crawl to walk to run, playing *PEW PEW* games. The men were eager to learn but clearly lacked the discipline that I had grown accustomed to in Ranger Battalion. Their feelings seemed to be easily hurt so it was necessary to adapt my tone so that they would be more receptive. This time gave me a greater appreciation for my Operational Detachment Alpha (ODA) counterparts, the Green Berets, who are responsible for training indigenous soldiers. It was a tough job to train the local forces.

If we spent three hours in the morning going over how and when to apply a tourniquet, there would be almost no retention after returning from lunch. I cannot speak with any great firsthand knowledge on the state of the public school system in Afghanistan, however, after seeing the lack of ability of these men to retain information and in conjunction with all that I have read on the topic, I would assume to say that something is failing. How important the early emphasis on building cognitive skills is because more and more apparent to me in these days. It wasn't that they weren't trying it was as though they just never downloaded the appropriate software to store the information.

As Christmas approached, we made contact with a reserve unit stationed at a small forward operating base (FOB) about five miles away. The post commander graciously invited us to have Christmas dinner with his unit, an invitation that we were most grateful for. The men that cooked in our tiny chow hall worked very hard for us but there is something very necessary about a larger gathering during these times. This was not my first Christmas in Afghanistan and to say that I missed my family was an understatement. On the short drive to the Army FOB, I allowed my mind to wander to my father's back porch where my siblings, nieces and nephews had inevitably gathered to share each other's company. There would no doubt be a couple of bottles of whiskey sitting out, all of my siblings' children were running and playing with their new toys, while all of the adults sat around the table and told stories and joked as the sun settled over the desert mountain range causing the sky to explode with a vibrant myriad of color and life.

Instantly, I was transported back to the tenebrous frigid reality of my current isolation as we approach the gate of the FOB. My heart was filled with gratitude as we were welcomed into the plywood dining hall. I had not realized it until then, but the look on my face was different than these soldiers. Although it had only been a couple of years since I wore the same uniform, I felt as though I had aged well beyond them. Their eyes did not seem at all heavy. I could somehow feel the weight of all the killing and surviving hanging from my face, my thick beard doing little to conceal its burden.

I thought back to 22 years old, sitting at a very similar table. As I took my seat, a slideshow of years at war, both overseas and with myself, rapidly flashed before me. I can see now that the tribulations endured during those fateful nights in Iraq while bringing violence to the den of the wolf paled in comparison to the affliction of parting ways with those that shared that experience. In that moment I knew that the worst of war that these men would ever endure would be that of leaving it behind.

With the exception of a couple of small earthquakes and nearly getting into a bar brawl with a group of German soldiers on their FOB on New Year's Eve, the remainder of our time in Konduz was pretty uneventful. We played soccer in the treacherous thick stones and I passed the time with wilted copies of works by Aristotle and Plato. During this month I still had been unable to contact my family. At this point, the only person in the US that even knew that I was back in a war zone was my father. I'm not sure why I protected this fact other than I already felt like a bit of a bastard for having put my family through what I later experienced when my former Battalion left for combat. I now knew what that felt like and had no desire to put my loved ones through it again. If they didn't know I was in harm's way, they wouldn't have to worry about me.

As it would be in some twisted dream, we sat in that same giant white diesel pickup truck on that same nearly deserted airfield in the middle of a blizzard waiting for our replacements. A quick hand off of the keys and a handshake and we were back on that small jet preparing to depart for Kabul. We wouldn't be staying in the capital long, however. I found out very quickly that a SOMC qualified medic in Afghanistan was a very in-demand position and I know had a little more freedom to move around the country.

One of the companies that we worked very closely with needed a medic to travel with them to Kandahar while they performed some low profile surveillance work. While there was some opportunity in Ranger Battalion to do things similar to this, it would have meant being pulled from the line, which in turn meant no direct action raids. That wasn't something that I was interested in at the time so I never pursued those particular jobs. This was different though. I was able to maintain my direct action status with the FAST team yet sort of sub in for some snoop and poop work.

A small element of bearded men boarded the small King Air jet with thick black pelican cases in tote. Arrangements had been made to stay in the overflow barracks of the Australian SAS soldiers at KAF (Kandahar Air Field). When we arrived it was my responsibility to make contact with the Officer in Charge (OIC) at the Combat Support Hospital (CSH-pronounced "CASH"). Although it wasn't something that we would broadcast, it was necessary that certain people knew that we would be operating in this area for the next few days. We showed our credentials to the appropriate people at the Joint Operations Center (JOC) and let them know the general area and time that we would be in their Area of Operations (AO).

So much of the difficulty in joint operations is that everyone seems to want to be the guy with the secret. People will only tell you little bits of information. More often than not, this isn't because anonymity is crucial for mission sanctity, it's because people want to feel cool. Due to this absurd ritual, we didn't give the guys with air support capabilities very much information and they didn't give the guys with an abundance of ground intel on the targets that they were hunting any. This is one of the reasons that wars drag on for as long as they do.

I had never been to Kandahar and was curious to look around. We would be going out early in the morning but had a few hours to check out the base. KAF had an outdoor mall with a roller hockey rink, I shit you not! There are sit down restaurants and shops and even an ice cream parlor! I couldn't help but sound like an old salty dog muttering something like, "Man back in the early days of the war we didn't have shit like this! Our entertainment was jerking off under the glow of a red head lamp in a porta shitter!"

The next morning I woke early, hovered over the toilet in a squat position for my morning glory, brushed my teeth using the water from a sealed plastic bottle, and admired my luscious beard in the reflection of the shined sheet metal that resembled a jailhouse mirror. I dressed in the light flowing garments of the local city clerks and switched from the bulky AK47 to a more streamlined MP5 in an effort to conceal the weapon under my tunic.

The commotion at the gate as we exit was customary. We got a few long looks from the gate guard as we exited in an old Afghan taxicab. There was a line of locals waiting to get on post in hopes of securing a day labor position. I've never worked the gate on a FOB before but I imagine that it is a terribly stressful job. Every person that approaches you is seemingly a friendly, hardworking human being that simply desires to make enough money to feed his family, however, that same individual may very well have enough explosive strapped to their person to eradicate you and everyone around you from the planet. I do not envy those young soldiers standing guard for hours on end, but the inquisitive look on each of their faces as we passed by suggested that they would have been happy to trade places.

Our driver was one of the NIU captains. He was trustworthy, not quite middle aged, and spoke decent English. I was sitting in the backseat on the passenger's side and our communications expert was sitting next to me. The team leader, a man named Dave, was riding shotgun. He was about 40 years old but didn't look over 25. Dave carried himself with a similar confidence yet with the relaxed demeanor of an expert surfer. He had spent his career in the US Special Operations, a resume that he never boasted but was evident by his knowledge and wherewithal.

Local police checkpoints were common throughout the country, especially in places of elevated concern such as in front of key buildings and bridges. In a military convoy we never really even slowed down for these types of obstructions. We would cruise by and wave politely but felt no need to stop. Today was different, however. We were as good as four locals getting a ride in a cab and would not be given a bye.

At a quick glance, we appeared normal enough but a longer look would reveal that we did not fit in. My tunic bulged slightly from the extra layer of armor that lay beneath. At one of these checkpoints, Dave rolled down his window as our dilapidated old car rumbled and puttered to a stop. In a rapid exchange, the local police officer and the would-be cab driver exchange words in as foreign to me as ancient Greek. The nature of our operation was secret. Anyone experienced in operations in this country knows that the local police knowing what is going on is analogous to calling the target and letting them know that you're coming.

The officer was not satisfied with the answers provided and leaned into the vehicle. The captain in the driver seat attempted to explain that he is NIU and showed his credentials. It wasn't enough to satisfy the curiosity of the officer. He pulled at the blanket wrapped around Dave's chest. In an almost cartoonish way, Dave slapped the man's fingers as if they had crept too close to the cookie jar. A crack of a smile is hidden by my beard until the man went back again for a second tug. Once again Dave slapped the officer's hand in an almost motherly fashion.

Now the rail thin man was more than just curious. He was determined to see what was going on under that blanket. He lunged into the window of the tiny car and grabbed at Dave's top. In a move that would impress Royce Gracie, Dave grabbed the man's wrist while simultaneously exposing the pistol hidden beneath the cover. Dave pulled the man halfway into the vehicle as he softly pushed the barrel of the firearm into the man's neck. Our comms chief yelled "GO" to the driver from the backseat.

His foot quickly transferred from the brake to the accelerator. We had just acquired a new passenger as the tires screeched and our car peeled out on the dirt road in front of the bridge ahead. The bottom half of the thin brown man in a grey wool uniform dangled from the taxi, kicking as we gained speed. His partner raised an AK47 but did not engage. I heard Dave say, "Is this, what you wanted to see? Is this what you were looking for?"

I looked beyond the front of the car to see the truck-mounted, Russian-made machine gun atop the green pick-up a hundred meters ahead. *Ohhh fuck!* Dave released his kung fu grip and left the gentlemen to execute a textbook barrel roll as we approached our inevitable doom at the hands of that hate-maker. To my absolute shock, we received little more than a perplexed look from the man standing at the helm of that weapon system as we flew by in a cloud of dust and nervous laughter. I looked back and looked back again. Nothing. Why didn't they radio to that guy? Why were we not just made into Swiss cheese?

"Fuck," was all Dave said as we settle back into our seats.

We make our way past several hut-like homes, the domicile of the nomadic sheep herders of South West Afghanistan. As if a light switch was tripped, we went from desolate farm lands into the chaotic hustle of a major city. Trade was alive and well in Kandahar as we passed by clerk after clerk peddling their goods to the city's inhabitants. No one was bothered by our presence, a circumstance that I was unaccustomed to. An interesting combination of anxiety and certainty settled over me. I understood fully that the reason for my perceived solace was strictly naivety, yet it somehow didn't matter.

The nature of the operation itself is still secret. In an effort to avoid committing a world-class operational security breach, I am going to omit a large part of the story here. I will say that the kabob that the NIU captain brought me for lunch was absolutely delicious. It was like a Mexican street taco on steroids.

Getting back on KAF was slightly more painstaking than leaving earlier that day. We tossed aside our blankets and affixed Velcro American flags to the strip of hook and pile tape on our body armor. A small American flag is placed on the dashboard to show our designation. We approached the gate slowly to be greeted by a tired, young Army private. He asked us to clear our weapons in the clearing barrel, I retorted in a smart-ass way that I don't know how to clear my fists in half buried container. He didn't smile.

Dinner was a Meal, Ready-to-Eat (MRE), as we just missed the open hours at the chow hall. Tomorrow we would be doing the same type of mission except we decided that it would behoove us to switch out vehicles. We acquired an old minivan from the Australians easily enough and found ourselves in bed rather early to get rest before tomorrow's objective. However instead of sleeping until morning, I awoke in the middle of the night with a pain in my gut that I have never before experienced. I leaped from my sleeping bag and sprinted for the closest latrine. It required every ounce of willpower that I possessed to not shit my pants. The contents of my abdomen exited like a bullet from a gun in one of the worst cases of splatter ass in the course of human history.

It was cold but I felt myself sweating. It doesn't take a Special Operations medic to know that this isn't a good situation. I moved quietly back into my bunk hoping to not disturb the other men in the room. I wasn't in my bed for more than a few minutes before I was called to duty again. *What is this?* It was like I swallowed hot coals! Everything was painful. I made a similar trip every thirty minutes until the sun came up.

When morning finally came, I slowly pulled myself out bed and tried to put myself back together in preparation for the day ahead of me. But as the other men were preparing for the upcoming operation, I was barely able to stand upright. I began swallowing Imodium like Tic-Tacs in an effort to attain mission readiness. I was the Doc and being sick was not an option. My responsibility was to these men and their safety and I would be climbing into that van regardless of my comfort level. The next ten hours were not fun.

I hadn't noticed how rutted out the road into the city was on the previous day. Curled up in the fetal position, every bump in the road felt like a prison shank to the gut. The pressure mounted in my bowels causing profuse sweating. The minutes felt like hours. More of my energy was being utilized to keep the contents of my intestines from saturating my pants than was spent pulling security on my sector. My discomfort wasn't what mattered though. Looking to the other men in the vehicle I knew I had to pull myself together. Eyes up. Stay alert. This is 'big boy' rules, there is no reset button and these men are depending on me. *Assemble strength. Focus.*

We made contact with our counterparts at the rally point. I forwent the typical formalities and quickly asked, "Is there a toilet I can use!" Saying that the conditions of the facility were terrible would imply that there was a facility at all. The shit spackled hole in the floor would have to do.

"You make it in time, Doc?" asked the burly former All American lineman for the Denver Broncos who was on the team.

"Haven't shit my pants since I was two, I'm not about to break that streak, brother!"

By the end of the third day of operations in Kandahar, we were finished and set to return to Kabul; I had lost 17 pounds and felt as near to death as I ever have. After we returned to the capital, I was invited back to conduct operations with that group and did so on countless occasions over the next few months. When Dave gave me a compliment about how reliable I was regardless of the severity of the situation, I couldn't help but think back on every employer that wouldn't give me a chance. I thought back to my experiences in a world that knew nothing of suffering for a greater good and felt a further sense of separation from their ranks. It's not to say that my actions were spectacular in the slightest. I acted the same way any one of my military brethren would have. I did my job under less than perfect conditions. This is how we conduct ourselves, yet this is not the picture that is painted upon our return.

Somehow, the American people have been handed a version of the combat veteran that includes a mentally broken, dejected, volatile mess. While I will admit that I could have been described as such more than once, it had little to do with my time in combat but rather the tribulation associated with the aforementioned stigma. I only became broken after hearing that I was broken from every potential employer, from the people at the VA and from every "you poor thing" face that I had to endure in the time after I left the Army. Here I was back in a war zone with no one dishing out pity or unnecessary empathy. Here I was with a group of guys that understood that we were just doing a job. Why can't the American people see that? Why are they so convinced that every veteran is a ticking time bomb?

Apparently it used to be customary in certain societies for there to be a sort of communal venting process when warriors returned from combat. The community would gather around and listen to the totality of what their protectors experienced in full detail. In doing so, the moral burden was dispensed throughout the entire population. No longer do we share the responsibility of such things. Not to oversimplify, but from an animalistic sense, killing is natural yet we have been told that it is the most unnatural, most unforgivable thing that a human can do to another. Yet during time of war we not only allow this act, we encourage it, we pay for it in dental and educational benefits, in medals and a set monthly salary. Then we, as a society, the ones who have encouraged the commission of such acts, turn a cold shoulder to those who we've asked to execute them. I am of the opinion that many individuals who believe that they are suffering from post traumatic stress are actually experiencing a form of cognitive dissonance associated with this social double standard. If killing is bad we should not pay our citizens to do it. If it isn't bad we shouldn't condemn those paid individuals for a job well done.

My time with the DEA as a private military contractor was short lived. I had the great fortune of conducting direct action raids at homes that acted as the root source for the financial support of the Taliban. We conducted low profile operations all over the country and had beers with some of the coolest bearded guys you will ever come across. Myself and a good friend named Tim ran directly across the tarmac of Kandahar International Airport one day, interrupting several flights, simply because we were bored. It was an exhilarating experience, one that to this day I am thankful for.

Despite how much I enjoyed what I was doing, I had become enamored with a young lady back home and was feeling more and more compelled each day to return to the States. It is certainly an interesting dichotomy, when you are home you seem to long for the familiarity and acceptance of the war zone. Sitting in the seeming stagnation of that place, thoughts of life passing you by back home flood your mind. Was war the ultimate realization of living life or the act of running from it?

When my team leader asked me to extend and stay in country for a few more months I simply and politely declined. I knew this lifestyle well enough to know that it isn't sustainable. You can only spin the cylinder of a revolver so many times in a game of Russian roulette before your luck runs out. More and more frequently we were taking risks that didn't need to be taken.

Returning from a combat zone is surreal in its own way. I can say that there is never a time in your life when your senses are as astute as in those first few days back on friendly soil. The air tastes different, the same songs that you have heard a hundred times before seem to sound better, and the food has a new flavor. The most notable difference for me has always been the roads. What would appear to be highly sporadic, reckless driving in the States is necessary for safety in places like Iraq and Afghanistan. Speed is security and you aren't tailgating until you have pushed the car in front of you off the road. The pavement is smooth at home. Add that to a very heavy right foot and there is a recipe for meeting all sorts of interesting individuals in uniform, not to mention scaring the living shit out of every one of your passengers.

I had lent my truck to one of the guys that I shared a house with at Purdue while I was away in return for a round trip ride to the airport. The first stop before even going home and dropping off my bag was to a pub that I enjoyed called, Nine Irish Brothers. The first order of business upon returning to the states is usually making up for all of the drunken shenanigans that I missed while I was away. I was able to get a few of my friends from the triathlon team to meet me for a late lunch and used all of my charm on them to stay and drink with me. Sadly, I have little charm and they all left after a single drink to write papers or study, or whatever good college students do on Tuesday afternoon. I, however, walked across the street to another, slightly seedier establishment and made my presence known by immediately proclaiming upon entering the front door, "Next round is on me!"

If you've ever been curious on how to make fifteen new friends with a single sentence, that's a good way to start. Doing that had been on my bucket list for some time and it felt good to check it off. It was like learning how to ride a motorcycle then riding to Vegas with my father immediately after my first deployment. Coming home truly makes you appreciate the little time that you have for such occasions. It eradicates the notion of, "I'll do it tomorrow." When you are in your twenties and have just returned from war, there is no such thing as tomorrow, you live hard and fast. Burning the candle at both ends doesn't seem to create the flame that you need so you search for another ignition point and another until you are reduced to a puddle of wax.

It's not that you're addicted to the sex, or alcohol, or intense exercise; it's more like you are challenging it out of a feeling of invincibility. *If war couldn't kill me then let's see what you're made of, whiskey! Let's see how much further I can push my body, my mind and my relationships. Let's burn it all just to see how close I can dance to the flame.*

I paid the $600 bar tab through half squinted eyes just before stumbling out into the early evening. In a sense, I paid for people to care about me for a moment. Nothing feels as lonely as the first time that you are without those who you have just been deployed. Nothing makes you feel as hollow and without hope as looking at the people around you laugh and joke without a care in the world when just 24 hours ago you carried two guns out of necessity. That feeling very quickly bleeds into loathing. I am not in any way boasting, in fact I hate the fact that I despise most people, I just don't feel like I belong to the human race anymore. The truth is. I kind of don't want to. People have such petty bullshit things that they call problems. I fully understand and respect that I have it pretty easy and that others have survived a great deal more suffering than I will ever be capable of comprehending, but the majority of problems that people complain about are completely in their head.

Chapter 10: Andria

"Namaste, motherfucker!" She shouted at me as I brought another round to our patio table.

She was already a little drunk. It was that feisty kind of drunk, more sassy than sloppy. Just the right amount. Andria couldn't have been more my type if I had the ability to create her in a laboratory. Her golden skin telling the story of her exotic Chinese and Hispanic heritage was taut around her small muscular build. She was a yoga teacher with a palpable love for life and adventure. Her infectious laughter filled the patio of the Irish pub that we sat at together and I knew this was it for me.

Our first date started just hours before at a costume store where we shopped for ninja outfits for a muddy buddy race that she had previously agreed to do with me. From there we sat for hours at a sushi restaurant drinking sake bombs and laughing like children as we became increasingly affected by the potent Japanese rice wine. We had just met but I knew that I had never in my life felt about anyone the way that I felt about her.

"I just love whiskey!" She exclaimed, interrupting my thoughts, as she brought the shot glass to her lips once more.

"We should go to Ireland than. They have lots of whiskey there, I'm told."

"I would love to go to Ireland someday."

"You want to go with me?"

"Hahaha! Yeah, sure, why not?"

I pulled my phone from my pocket as she continued. "I'm done with school at the end of August, that would be a good time I think."

"I was thinking like Monday."

"Hahaha! Yeah, sure, why not!?"

Discreetly scrolling through the deals on a travel website I asked her again, "Really? You want to go with me?"

"Fuck it! Hahaha! Let's go!"

I pulled my credit card from my wallet and asked her, "Window or aisle?"

"Hahaha! I don't care, whatever."

She must have thought that I was joking because she was in disbelief when I showed her the confirmation for two round trip tickets and a rental car.

We stumbled through the deserted city streets after the bar closed. It was that awkward part of the night where the air is filled with a very specific anxious uncertainty. You begin to replay all of the highlights of a great first date. She laughed at my jokes. It felt like there was chemistry but I didn't want to overstep. I didn't want to understep either. *If you make a move and it was too soon, you risk scaring her off. If you wait too long, she is going to think you are uninterested. Is she waiting for you to make a move, or is she just thinking about getting home and going to bed?* In that moment, I was only partially present for the conversation and tripping over my own words like an adolescent having his first encounter with a long time crush. It's funny how no matter how much confidence we as men have from all we have accomplished, the right girl somehow has the ability to deconstruct it all with a single look.

The pace was little more than a casual stroll but my heart beat was acting like I just ran into a firefight in Iraq. At the moment that I decided what to do, Andria partially tripped over a grate in the sidewalk and conveniently fell into me resulting in what I hoped would be my last long first kiss.

We went back to her place and as we began to fool around, she fell asleep. I mean she completely passed out. Snoring, the whole deal. I had to laugh. It was somehow the sweetest thing I had seen. She just... *fell asleep.* The next day I awoke by her side to the sound of her phone ringing. It was her mother checking up on her.

Very few things are as uncomfortable as laying in a bed next to a girl that you just had a first date with while she has a conversation with her mother. It's like her mom knows that you are there and hates you.

After a quick breakfast, we donned our ninja gear and headed toward the muddy buddy race with Andria's roommates. We had entered in the 'Two Person Contest' division. My intention was to just have fun and not be concerned about the race itself. That lasted until about three seconds after they said, "Go!" At what I felt was a leisurely pace, we began passing most of the other competitors. I realized after about a half of a mile that we were getting close to the front of the pack and got incredibly excited at the idea of winning this race. To her credit, Andria kept up with the pace that I was now setting in an effort to pass the leaders for the first mile or so. When she started to back off a little, we risked losing ground, and I was not okay with that. As though it was some kind of combat obstacle course, I scooped the 5'3", 110 lb yoga instructor up and began navigating through the trees like *Forrest Gump* taking Lieutenant Dan to safety.

We passed two more teams like this before coming to a river crossing. I set her down and we managed to get closer to the final team in front of us. I knew the finish line was not that far away and we had them in our sights. I noticed something right then. She didn't care about winning like I did. She just wanted to have fun. Something clicked in me at that moment. Her happiness was way more important than winning a race. That may not seem like much of a revelation for most people, but it struck me like a bolt of lightning. A little over a half a mile later became the first time I was ever completely okay with coming in second. I won the minute we started that race together. I didn't realize it then, but I did when I saw her smile when we crossed the finish line.

For the next couple of days we didn't leave each other's sight. Our first date continued on. I met her mother when she gave us a ride to the airport. I laughed when she told me that she wanted to take a DNA sample before getting on the plane with her daughter. I stopped laughing when she pulled out a swab and container at the curbside drop off and asked me to open my mouth. She was serious! She legitimately had the kit to take my DNA!

We boarded the flight and our first date would continue for another week as we drove in one a giant circle around the entire island of Ireland. We explored like two children dropped off in a mysterious new world. Just the act of attempting to leave the parking lot left us laughing uncontrollably. For starters I had not driven a manual for years and now I had to adapt to a left-handed stick shift. The seizure like movement resulting from my inexperience was terribly amusing to Andria as she kicked her head back in a fit of laughter at my struggle.

We spent the first night exploring the bars of Dublin. After more whiskey than any two people should be allowed to consume, Andria had her heart set on pulling off the acrobatic lift maneuver from dirty dancing. The celluloid moment that captured the hearts of a generation of teenage girls, convincing them that they too would someday be swept off their feet, is not intended to be performed with a blood alcohol level in the double digits. What was intended to be a graceful display of athleticism looked more like the hit a linebacker puts on a rookie quarterback on third and long.

The next morning we decided to head south toward the Blarney Castle. At the time I didn't know much about the Blarney Stone, just that it was a popular tourist destination in Ireland. As we walked through the parking lot I couldn't help but overhear the excitement in an elderly couple's conversation about finally being able to visit this place. Not thinking much about it, Andria and I navigated the steep winding cobblestone staircase to the top of the castle for our turn get to first base with a giant rock.

After descending to the base of the castle, I noticed the elderly couple sitting on a bench outside. I heard the man say, "I'm not going to leave you here. This is close enough for me."

"That's silly" she responded. "Just because I can't make it up those steps doesn't mean you shouldn't see it. We've waited our entire lives for this."

"That's exactly what it means. I'm happy to sit here with you and enjoy the view."

It is amazing how overhearing such a short conversation can alter the way that you approach life. I didn't know their back story but what I heard was *don't wait to live your life*. When it comes to happiness, sometimes you have to throw caution to the wind and grab life with both hands. No one else is going to experience it for you; it's up to you to live the shit out of it. Seeing two people spend a lifetime wanting something but waiting until it was safe, getting so close and having to sit there and watch a hundred other people live out their dream altered my perspective. Looking at the way the setting sun was dancing on Andria's hair I couldn't help but be thankful that I had decided to leave Afghanistan.

We departed the Blarney Castle in route to the Cliffs of Moher, stopping off in Cork along the way. Once again we found ourselves stumbling through the streets exploring the various old bar and winding stone roads. Every moment seemingly better than the one before. We experienced the cliffs at sunset and stayed in quaint road side bed and breakfasts. By day four, we linked up with a group of locals at a local rock climbing festival. Our first home together was the tent that we shared, overlooking the cliffs of Northern Ireland. By day six, we were in Bushmill sipping whiskey and cloves. Pushing the limits of the little rental car, we managed to visit the Bushmill and Jameson distillery on the same day to conclude our tour of an incredible island. There was no plan or itinerary, just two people losing themselves in one another. What would have seemed excessive to any other person that I had ever been with was a challenge to Andria. From that point forward, no one else seemed to exist on her level.

Even the best first dates have to come to an end and this one was no different. When we got back to the States, she returned to a full schedule of work and school and I set out to tie up a few loose ends from before my deployment to Afghanistan. Not a day went by when we didn't talk to each other in some way. Our conversations nearly always turned into planning lavish adventures. We had always been, on our own, each a stream of gasoline. When our rivers converged they sparked a flame that erupted the world in a sanguine spectrum of color and opulent warmth. I loved her from the first day I saw her.

Chapter 11: Scenes from Highways

My deployment as a medic for the DEA in Afghanistan did a lot of things for me. For starters, it put a decent amount of money in my pocket. It was the first time in my adult life that I actually had a real savings account. In addition to my newfound financial freedom, I remembered just how big the world is and how little of it I had seen, relatively speaking. I knew that I no longer wanted to make a career out of federal law enforcement, making my course of study at Purdue obsolete, and I knew that I didn't want to be in Indiana any longer.

Being back in a war zone reminded me of how finite the days of our lives are. It reminded me of the promise that I made to James Regan after he died that I wouldn't waste so much as a single day on this planet being unhappy if I could do something about it. Combine all of that with having just met Andria, and a perfect storm arose that tore apart the blueprint of what my life was supposed to look like.

I left the city where Andria and I met to return to West Lafayette, Indiana. I felt out of place there before but now it was much more than just social discomfort. I heard another life calling me somewhere else, anywhere else but there. In the summer of 2009, with less than a half a dozen classes left in my degree, I left Indiana. I felt that I learned all that I could from that place; I had grown beyond it. I spent weeks traveling around the country catching up with family and old friends, all the while keeping in touch with Andria through long phone conversations and random weekends dropping in to see her.

The two of us took a ten-day trip to Costa Rica that summer that we called our second date. When we tried to drive into Panama to go rock climbing, we were stopped by the police and kicked out of the country for being undocumented. One early morning, as the sun was rising over Jaco, we had a near death experience as a giant crocodile decided to investigate the two of us bobbing on our surfboards just past where the waves were breaking. Together we explored another part of the world, leaping into the vast ocean and kissing beneath the most picturesque tropical waterfalls imaginable.

I wasn't sure what my future held, and as long as I was holding her in it, I didn't care. We talked endlessly about continuing the adventure forever. We discussed moving to New Zealand and working on a llama farm. We researched the best way to move to Thailand as U.S. citizens and all the places that we wanted to go together and the food we would eat when we got there, and all of the endless adventures between now and our final days. Just a few months after our first date we settled on Colorado as the perfect place to go. When we returned from Costa Rica, I spent a couple of weeks making the arrangements for the two of us to move there together. The plan was for me to arrive in Lakewood, Colorado two weeks before Andria and get everything set up.

Once again, I found myself driving across the country in my old pick up with Jameson in the passenger seat. More corn fields. More time to think. My mind began to drift back to another long road trip that I had taken five years before. It was the final week of the Special Operations Medical Course when four of us piled into that same Dodge Dakota and drove from Fort Bragg North Carolina to Boston Massachusetts.

Jess, Chris, Kenny and I all piled into my little extended cab Dakota for what we considered would be the last time that we would see each other. We were going to different Battalions after graduation and knew that meant moving on. We decided to spend one last epic weekend together

We were four, early twenty year old, barrel chested freedom fighters with a couple of hundred dollars in our pockets. Our first stop was the nation's capital. It didn't take long to realize that we couldn't afford the drinks that we were buying. Hell, we couldn't even afford a hotel room. We parked my Dakota in a ten story parking garage for $16 and planned on sleeping in the truck that night. Just before we were thrown out of the second bar we decided to take advantage of the opportunity to take a midnight tour of the capital. We stuffed our cargo pockets with cans of cheap beer that we bought at a liquor store and made our way to the mall area.

Our boisterous laughing came to a screeching halt as we approached the Vietnam memorial. It was the middle of the night and we were the only four souls there yet we felt the presence of nearly 60,000 fellow veterans. A lightning bolt shot up my spine as I saw the magnitude of the structure. I believe that each of us, in that moment, gained a much greater understanding of what we had embarked upon. We would all take our first steps off the back ramp of an Air Force cargo plane onto hostile ground in the coming months. A journey that we each looked forward to but this moment would hang in our consciousness through each of those crucial steps. In many ways we were becoming the legacy of every one of those names.

Moving on, we pulled the lukewarm beer from our pockets and enjoyed the solitude of one of the nation's busiest cities. The orchestra of crickets performed the soundtrack to the end of our first evening of uninhibited freedom. We made our way back to the parking garage. Chris and Kenny opted to sleep in the bed of the truck and Jess and I put the front seats in full recline. Sometime just before sunrise we surrendered to the fatigue of a long week of training. As the stream of cars entered the parking structure on Friday morning their screeching tires served as our alarm clock. Jess and I exit the cab to stretch and hear Chris complaining of a terrible headache. Kenny chimes in and mentions his head aches as well. At first I think that they may be hung over but then start laughing. When they ask what is so funny, the words, "carbon monoxide poisoning," barely escaped as my laughter filled the garage.

In a very similar way that we explored DC we laughed and joked and saw the sights. The bull on Wall Street and a distant Statue of Liberty stood out as beacons of what we would be fighting for in the days to come but when we approached the cavernous abyss that was formerly the World Trade Center a tidal wave of sorrow and purpose crashed over us. Giving yourself to a cause is one thing but to see the smoldering village that has brought your countrymen to arms stirs something in a warrior's soul that no blade can defeat. The emotional dissonance was deafening. The pain, the hate, the sorrow and rage all swirled together in a tornado of sensation. My hands trembled, a tear wanted to roll from my eye but it would not. Instead, I felt my fist clench with such force that my nails broke the skin of my palms.

This moment may very well have been the foundation of all the callous vengeful actions that my hands would carry out on the field of battle. This sight before me, a place where thousands of innocent people were murdered would become my justification for every inhuman act that I perpetrated on behalf of my people. I am not the type of man who has ever in his life started a fight, yet the site of such tragedy boiled the blood in my veins, an act that demanded consequence. A man is of little worth if he is unwilling to end those who commit atrocities against his home.

Not a word was spoken as the four young Army Rangers made their way back to the truck. It wasn't rage that consumed us, it was a renewed sense of purpose. Even before this we were four of the most motivated young men you were likely to meet, but this day taunted our resolve. It became the first of many weights that we each postured to carry.

With the windows down and the music up we were as free on that road as any of us had ever been. We had little knowledge of the hardships that we would encounter in the months and years to come. We were free and clear of the albatross of war, the burden of surviving the death that would drip from each of our fingertips. Life was easy and the gas was cheap, so we rolled on embracing all that our nation provided to us.

Without a plan, Jess suggested a Red Sox/Yankees game at Fenway in Boston. I had always wanted to see a Yankees game and to see one at Fenway Park would be amazing. I was on board with the idea immediately. We decided collectively that purchasing Yankees hats for the day's game at Fenway would be an outstanding idea.

"You sure about this?" asked the gentlemen from behind the counter at the souvenir shop. Within ten steps of exiting the small gift shop we were welcomed on the street with a slew of obscenities and insults. Apparently, they REALLY don't like the Yankees there.

We were a hundred feet from the stadium and began inquiring what the cost of tickets would be from a scalper. The price for cheap seats was more than any of us made in a week, a fact that each of us expected but was still discouraged by. We decided that the bar directly across the street would be the best place to watch the game. We cheered obnoxiously whenever the away team got on base and received an outpour of enthusiasm when the home team scored. We heard a lot more cheers than boos over the next hour, a fact that in all honesty likely kept us safe. Had the Yankees pulled ahead at any point, we likely would have been in real trouble.

We shuffled from one bar to another, meeting various people and hearing over and over how stupid we were for wearing Yankees hats in this neighborhood. None of the aggressive comments were at all bothersome until a clergyman in all black with a white collar told us in a thick accent, "You'se guys betta take dem hats off or something bad's about to happen to youse."

Never been threatened by a priest before, so we can check that off the list, I thought to myself as we created distance from the priest.

As the final inning came to a close we stumbled into one last bar welcomed by dozens of locals laughing at us and the sorry effort of our team. It didn't take long for one surly young gentleman to enter my comfort zone and begin bombarding me with a series of, "How dares youse?" and "Da faq is dat shit on yer head?" My back was firmly against the bar so I didn't have to worry about one of his friends hitting me from behind. I waited patiently as Jess, Chris and Kenny put themselves in position around the drunk twenty something year old. I stood in silence as he berated me in what was almost a foreign language.

By the time he paused each of my friends had quietly placed themselves within a foot of the man. I asked him as calm as possible, "Do you know what an Army Ranger is?" His eyes opened fully for the first time and quickly looked left and right as I did. He realized that while he was in the midst of his vulgar vituperation that four men who genuinely enjoyed violence had surround him. His pause was short before proclaiming, "Youse guys is in da Aamy? Ahh shit! Why didn't ya say so.... Ahh Mick, get these guys a drink on me eh!" And like that we went from sworn enemies to best friends. My would-be assailant turned and hollered at a couple of other friends, "HEY... dees guys is Aamy guys!" We didn't pay for another drink all night.

My thoughts returned to the long stretch of road still ahead of me in route to Colorado. I thought back to that guy with the thick Boston accent in the pub outside of Fenway five years earlier in 2004. At the time none of us had really done anything to earn the goodwill that he showed to us that night. In a sense he was lazy with his gratitude. At the time, all that any of us had managed to do was survive a year and a half of military schools and yet we were treated like heroes. Questions that I couldn't answer began to creep into my brain as the mile markers zipped by on I-70 westbound.

To what degree should civilians have knowledge of the actions of the military? In Special Operations, we resided under a blanket of operational security; we were not allowed to tell non-essential personnel about what we were doing due to the potential of compromising a mission or the people conducting it. Is the lack of transparency from the military partially to blame for the ignorance of its nation's civilians? Or is the social obligation to have at least some knowledge of how the military operates on those being protected by it?

Those questions went largely unanswered in my mind as the wild, expansive Rocky Mountains broke the horizon and shattered the monotony of the long flat road I had been on for what seemed like days. Jameson had been asleep for eight straight hours, but I had to wake her so she could see how magnificent it was. She was only mildly impressed and returned to her resting position as soon as I allowed it.

Sight unseen, I had secured an apartment at the base of Green Mountain. It was modest by a modest person's account, but it was a fresh new start in a place that I had always wanted to live. It would be another two weeks before my girlfriend arrived so Jameson and I set out on a mission to explore the neighborhood. The only person I knew in the state would normally have lived about forty minutes away in Boulder, but at the time he was on contract with Blackwater. I was, for the time, alone in a new strange place, not that it bothered me terribly. The military taught me how to quickly adjust to new environments. It was foreign and exciting, and would soon be the first time I ever lived with someone I was dating.

Chapter 12: Safer In the Forest

Jameson and I hit the ground running. Well, I hit the ground running. She spent most of her time napping on the patio of our second floor apartment. I submitted updated resumes and applications to dozens of local jobs, but once again heard nothing back. I masked the disappointment of those minor rejections with training. I was getting better at the sport of triathlon by this time. I was learning to take my feelings of pain and anger and rejection out on the pedals of my bike. In the professional world, I wasn't taken seriously; but on a race course I could pass any CEO or other affluent member of society. My athleticism became an equalizer.

As a result I became increasingly obsessed with the sport of triathlon. I spent upwards of forty hours per week training. I trained so much that by the end of September, I came down with pneumonia. Despite being very ill, I competed in a half-ironman race and a full marathon on back-to-back weekends. Both of which I placed second in my respective category, and in the top two-percent overall.

I couldn't stop. I had to train more, I had to race more. Andria had arrived, making it one of the happiest times of my adult life but my need to train quickly became a wedge between her and I. She spent much of her time doing yoga but nowhere near the time that I spent training. She couldn't understand why I was going on multiple 5+ hour bike rides every week, or why I was spending so much on new bike parts. To be honest neither did I. I didn't even have a job so spending $400 on a set of pedals was asinine. I had to go faster. I had to go longer and harder. I had to prove my self-worth in one way or another.

I had lost nearly twenty pounds since returning from Afghanistan in the late spring, yet my compulsion led me to want to run longer and farther. As long as I was running, I wasn't feeling, so I ran. I ran until my feet bled because the last thing that I wanted to do was face the demons of my past. This was supposed to be a new start. This was supposed to be the beginning of my happy family but no matter where I was, those same memories seemed to track me down.

On the surface, life seemed to be going well because I wasn't being honest with myself about the pain that I was in. One fall evening, Andria and I were enjoying a quiet night at home together. Jameson paced somewhat nervously around the apartment uncharacteristically. She walked to the front door and looked back at us on the couch. Out of nowhere, a stream of blood violently jettisoned from her backside.

It was like a scene out of the exorcist. The bloody puddle covered the ground surrounding her. I had never seen anything like it. In all the bloodshed that I had seen as a medic in Iraq and Afghanistan, nothing could have prepared me for seeing that. What was worse was I couldn't ask her what was wrong.

We immediately searched for a 24-hour veterinary clinic nearby and as soon as we found one, loaded her in the car. Andria drove while I held Jameson in my lap in the back seat. She was motionless and covered in blood. I was covered in blood. She didn't deserve this. She just kept looking at me. I'd seen that look before. That was the, *I'm dying* look. It never crushed me when I saw it in another person the way it did when I saw it in her fading brown eyes.

As we entered the front door of the clinic she exploded again. The dark red blood set a stark contrast to the bright white tiles of the establishment's floor. I felt completely helpless. Had it been a person, I would have at least had some clue of what to do but all I could do now was put her in the care of the clinic staff. We were not allowed to stay after we admitted her. We returned home to clean up the blood that had begun to stain the entranceway of our new apartment. I washed my buddy's blood from my arms one more time and hopped that she was in competent hands.

Two days later we were able to take Jameson home. She looked absolutely exhausted but somehow smiled in her own way. I gladly paid the $2,000 vet bill and Andria took to making her chicken and brown rice per the doctor's suggestion. Apparently Jameson had contracted a severe case of Giardia, which is single cell parasite that can affect the intestinal tract of dogs.

After a few months, I finally settled for a job at an outdoor store that was better than nothing. It only paid nine dollars an hour but I was happy to have the opportunity. I would be selling snowboards, a job that I was familiar with and looked forward to. On the first day, the manager had me organizing golf balls, something that I knew absolutely nothing about but wasn't going to argue. After about an hour, he told me that I wasn't allowed to wear a hat and that I had to take it off. A statement that I thought was clearly a joke as he was wearing a Titleist ball cap. I had on a beanie from a popular snowboarding company and thought it quite appropriate seeing as how my job was to sell their products. When I chuckled thinking it was a joke, he quickly informed me that it wasn't. Okay, I thought, not like the last place you worked but it's cool. I will just take off my hat and go back to the mind numbing activity of organizing these stupid little white balls.

Swallow that pride. About ten minutes, later the same guy came up and told me that I had to tuck my shirt in. It was a brown Volcom button down shirt with a collar, an article of clothing that would have been considered dressing up at the last shop that I worked for. I looked at the black Ping polo shirt that he was wearing and noticed that it was not even a little tucked in. Okay, he's fucking with me. "Roger that, sir" I reply and untuck my shirt as soon as he walks away.

"I wouldn't do that." Whispered my 17-year-old colleague who was showing me the difference between a driver and a wedge.

"He's not serious?" I replied.

"Oh no he's a dick. That's how he is to everyone, especially new people."

I thought back to the Ranger Regiment. When we were at the range and the chow truck finally came with food, the lowest ranking members of the platoon always ate first. The line was formed in ascending order from lowest to highest rank. That way if we ran out of food the most senior guys were the ones that didn't eat. That was called leading from the front. That was showing the guys that put out so much effort for you that they would not go without. That form of leadership is real. It isn't some truncated version based off of whose daddy owned the shop. My blood began to boil when I thought of having to be led by this guy. He didn't have the slightest clue how to lead men. He was used to cracking a whip at teenagers and laughing while they hopped-to. I wasn't a teenager. I'm a combat veteran with multiple combat deployments in Special Operations!

The chip on my shoulder swelled. I saw him barking at two other employees about how to move a rack and realized that he hadn't actually done anything all day. The urge to walk over and punch him in the face grew in me like the heat from a jet engine taking off. I turned and walked toward the door. "You taking a lunch, Leo?" Asked the young kid behind the register.

"Yeah something like that." I replied. I had no intention of ever stepping foot in that place again. I wasn't a teenager and I wasn't about to be treated like one. I had earned the respect of some of the greatest men of our generation and I'm sure that over time I would have earned his, but the fact is, I didn't want it. I didn't want anything to do with a fat lazy piece of shit like that. I didn't want him going home and bragging that he has a former Ranger working for him. Was this the world that I was supposed to be integrating back into? Why the fuck should I have to capitulate to a man of a noticeably lower caliber?

I returned home angry and defeated. On the way, I stopped off and picked up a bottle of whiskey and indulged in the serenity of the numbness that it provided. I was 26 years old and had done more, and accomplished greater things in the past six years than most men will in a lifetime yet in my mind, I was a puzzle piece that didn't fit anywhere. Those same experiences that I felt made me a crown jewel in the job market were the very qualities that alienated me from it. Was it possible that I was affixing a greater worth to the things that I had done or was this nation's priorities completely upside down? What kind of society asks a strong man to take a backseat to a weak one?

It wouldn't be long before I had another retail job. It wasn't ideal but was better than the three rejections a week that I had been receiving from other companies. It was about an hour round trip commute for shifts that often lasted only four hours. At first, the job was a lot of fun and I was treated well by my fellow employees. The average age at this shop was a little older than the previous one so I didn't feel too out of place. It wasn't until I came under a surprise review from the store's general manager a few months after starting that there was any issue. Employees received incredible discounts on just about every type of gear imaginable so I went a little overboard at first.

I had a lot of money saved up when I moved to Colorado and spent a nice chunk of it on new bike parts, snowboard and camping gear. This apparently raised a few red flags. I was pulled into the GM's office and was basically told that since there is no way that I could afford so much stuff on my salary that I must be buying it and selling it on the side, which was very much against the rules. Like the manager of the previous shop, he knew my background. He knew that I was a combat veteran and that I served in my time in the Army as a Ranger. Although, he likely didn't know what being a Ranger actually meant. Aside from having the word "HONOR" tattooed in large black block letters on my left arm, I always attempt to conduct myself in a way indicative of a person of high moral character and integrity. This gentleman was, for all intents and purposes, calling me a thief. This was a designation that I absolutely did not care for.

The idea that I would compromise my own personal code of conduct to make a couple hundred dollars was beyond insulting. The true root of the problem was that this person, like many in our great nation, did not possess anything resembling a clue as to what a Ranger is, or a SEAL or a PJ or a Recon Marine or a member of Special Forces or a member of any of our armed services for that matter. He was never told, or bothered to learn on his own, that the type of person who commits their entire life to a cause is not typically the type of person to rip off a store for a couple hundred dollars worth of gear. I can't say comprehensively that every single member of the military exudes altruism, however, to question my integrity without provocation was upsetting to say the least.

I don't believe that the implication that I was a thief bothered me as much as the fact that this person didn't care to know about what I was willing to give up for him. Before I ever met this man, I vowed to keep him safe, to die for him if need be in a land that he will never get within a thousand miles of. He, and the rest of society, doesn't want to hear that. It's likely not even something that a person of his particular caliber is capable of comprehending. Yet here I was having to answer to him. I had to explain why I bought eight different pairs of running shoes in two months. What could I say to appease his ignorance? *Sir, I run every night while you sleep because I am haunted by the deaths of more people than I can count...so I go through a lot of shoes.*

When I explained to him that I made a significant amount more at my previous job, that I had not always been a stock boy, and that calling me a thief was a very good way to get a massive HR complaint dropped on his head, he changed his tone quickly. It was a breaking point though. I couldn't keep doing this. I couldn't keep having a person that couldn't walk a mile in my shoes continue to be in a position over me. I had been spoiled by some of the best leaders in our nation. The kind of person that it takes to be in a supervisory position in Special Operations is as far separated from the managers in the civilian world, as a kindergartner is from a Doctor.

By this time, my friend Jess had left his job in Pennsylvania and moved to Colorado. I insisted that he stay with me in the guest bedroom of my new home in Golden. He seemed very appreciative, but to be honest, his was a welcome presence for me. It was great to have my old training partner back under the same roof. We had done our first CrossFit workout together over six years before while at the Special Operations Medical Course. Jess brought some of his gear and we set up a small gym in the garage. I don't think that he was ever as competitive with me as I was with him, but I know that both of us worked harder when the other person was around. Before we knew it, we had a couple of other people coming over and training with us. The one car garage was cramped with two squat racks and two row machines.

One day on my way to swim I saw a For Rent sign in the window of a local business. I had driven by at least a hundred times and had never noticed the sign before that day. I called the number on the sign from the parking lot. As fate would have it, the owner was actually inside the building. He invited me in and showed me around. My mind immediately imagined what the place would look like with mats on the floor and pull up bars hanging from the ceiling. Knowing that I couldn't afford it, I asked how much the rent was. When he told me, I replied, "PER MONTH?"

I think that he believed that I felt it was overpriced when I was actually surprised at how inexpensive it was. He immediately countered and offered a lower price. This is doable I thought. If each of the people that are already working out with us in the garage paid a little over a hundred a month, this place would already be paid for. I asked the gentleman a series of questions attempting to not sound overly excited.

This could be it. This could be my ticket to not having to take orders from a person who didn't give a damn about me. My entire swim that day was spent calculating the cost of opening my own gym. When I got home I mentioned it to my girlfriend. She had always dreamed of having her own yoga studio to teach at and this could very much be it. Initially, it seemed like she didn't quite believe that it was possible until about two days later when I had a signed lease in my hand. I remember coming home and telling her that she had her own studio now. It was the happiest that I had seen her the entire time that we were together.

The process of converting the space was fast. We only lived about a half mile away so getting the equipment moved was easy. We painted the walls and got flooring from a horse supply shop on the other side of Denver. In total, I spent about $3,000 to get the rest of what I needed. I told my direct supervisor at the shop where I worked that I was going to be starting my own business, but still wanted to work there part-time. I told him that I could really only handle ten to fifteen hours a week for the first couple of months while the gym was getting started, a number that he agreed would be fine. He praised me for my ingenuity and willingness to go after my goals. He said that the company supported its employees in pursuing their dreams.

The week that my gym opened, I was put on the schedule at the shop for forty hours. There must be some mistake, I thought. When I approached the very same manager that told me that ten to fifteen hours a week wouldn't be a problem, he said that he wasn't doing the scheduling anymore. He advised me to just get someone else to take over the shifts and that it wouldn't be a problem. It was a problem. The company refused to let anyone take the shifts because everyone was already working forty hours that week because of a big sale.

This left me at a crossroad. I really couldn't afford to have someone else at my new business the first week it was open, but I couldn't exactly call in sick. They knew that I needed the time off but didn't seem to care. The time came when I had to be in two places at once. I was on the schedule at the shop and had to coach a class at the same time. My phone rang at 11:30 that morning. It was the same manager that told me that reducing my hours wouldn't be a problem at all.

"Hey Leo, I'm not sure if you knew it but you were scheduled for the morning shift today not the afternoon shift."

"Yeah, I know."

"Oh okay, good. So then you're coming in then."

"Nope, sure as shit not!"

"Well when we discussed this you said that you were going to be here for the team. It's a busy sales day."

"Yup, but I'm not. So how does that feel? How does it feel when someone says that they are going to be there to help you out, that they have your back, and then they fail to come through? How does that shit feel?"

"Okay, have a good day, then."

Andria just grinned at me in that kind of, *that is why I love you* sort of way as she left for work. Had the general manager treated me with respect, I would likely still be affiliated in some way with the company. Instead I decided to resign my position making $10 an hour to pave my own way in the world and become my own boss.

Chapter 13: A Broken Jar

It was the summer of 2010 and I had just opened my first business. It was 1,600 modest square feet, sandwiched between a machine shop and Mexican restaurant. One of my best friends was living in my guest bedroom, Jameson had made a full recovery, my triathlon conditioning was better than it had ever been, and my girlfriend and I were getting along great.

I had already competed in a half a dozen races that season and was beginning to really find my rhythm. In a very uncharacteristic fashion, I decided to go on a somewhat leisurely bike ride. I had already done my two training events for the day but I was feeling great and my girlfriend was in Boulder with some friends. About thirty minutes into the ride, I was traveling on a long straight away at just under thirty miles per hour when a person in the passenger seat of a white car reached out the window and pushed me off the road. To this day I do not know what provoked them to do so.

The thin front wheel of my Specialized Tarmac buried itself into the soft dirt shoulder. The bike went left and I went right as my body instinctively tucked itself in preparation for impact. I tasted dirt on my tongue, as my body met the ground the way a heavyweight fighter's glove meets his opponent's face. As soon as the dust settled, I attempted to sit up. A couple that was passing by had seen what had happened and stopped. The man told me not to move. *I'm good*, I thought.

"I gotta ride home." I told him.

"No, I think maybe you better stay still until the ambulance comes." He replied to me. I just laughed. I don't need an ambulance. I'm a medic. I don't need a medic. I wanted to walk it off. A poor decision considering my right collarbone had been rearranged into the shape of a lightning bold and my hip was broken.

I got to joke with the paramedic the whole way to the hospital about how he didn't have the balls to give me all the fentanyl in the box. When he cut away my jersey and saw the Ranger Medic crest tattooed on my ribs, he returned fire and told me that he may need to intubate to shut me up. I appreciated his humor more than any of the drugs that he provided. It brought me back to all the times that I worked on one of my guys and tried desperately to make them laugh. If there was one thing that I felt made for a good medic, it was someone that could not only be calm themselves but take their patent's mind away from the pain.

I arrived at the hospital in good spirits. I was able to call my girlfriend and tell her not to worry that I got in a little accident. The firemen joking about how messed up I was in the background likely didn't help the tone of the message. She came and sat by my side in the emergency room, making jokes to lighten the mood. Several hours later, I was released and she drove me home. I was in a considerable amount of pain and didn't know what to do with myself. My clavicle had broken in such a way that it created a massive bulge under my skin. It felt as though the bone could tear through the thin skin at any time; I could feel it grinding just beneath the surface. I didn't have insurance at the time because I had just left my job to start my business. I knew that I could go to the VA but I wasn't sure the extent of what they could provide.

I was told that they could affix a plate to the bone holding it in place. However, since I wasn't registered with the regional VA, I would have to go through a health care screening first. The idea of getting this thing fixed was all I could think about and gladly agreed to the screening. I had to do a general medical and psychological screening which included filling out a few forms. On the psych form there was a series of questions including, *Have you ever been deployed to a combat zone?* Yes. *Have you ever discharged your weapon at an enemy combatant?* Yes. *Have you ever killed an enemy combatant?* Yes. *Have you ever seen a dead U.S. service member?* Yes.

The questions kept going on like this and I kept checking the yes box, a fact that apparently qualified me for a meeting with a couple of mental health specialists. Before that moment, I don't think I really ever thought of myself as being a person with any type of mental health issue.

The guys I worked with in my early twenties did all of the same things that I did and they were all fine. Or I assumed that they were all fine. Sure we would drink a bottle of whiskey and put our fist through the wall from time to time, but that didn't seem abnormal. That was just who we were. I was guided down the hall to a tiny room with two women standing inside. The two women in the stuffy room illuminated by a buzzing fluorescent light talked to me like they were the school nurse and I was a kid that just scraped my knee. It felt terribly condescending, like my mind was broken and needed fixing. My mind is fine I thought, it's my shoulder that looks like a question mark. I dismissed pretty much all of what they had to say, mainly because of the way that they said it to me. I wasn't about to let two women lecture me about what combat stress can do to me. What the fuck did they know about combat stress? Oh, they read a book about it while enjoying their iced orange-mocha frappuccino in their air conditioned college dorm room, *please go on and enlighten me, Doctor.*

I scheduled the surgery at the next available time, which was over a week later. I lay on the couch sucking back pain pills and whiskey like Tic-Tacs and Kool-Aid. My Ranger buddy and former college roommate, Matt, sent me legit frozen deep-dish pizza from Chicago and Jess and his wife Anna took turns checking on me. Along with my girlfriend, they helped cover the classes at the gym and kept it running while I was down. If it hadn't been for them, that business never would have survived its second month. They never once asked for anything in return, just that I get better. Those kinds of friends are priceless; those kinds of friends are family.

When I awoke from the procedure at the VA, I recall being in a bit of pain. I asked the nurse if she could help with pain management but she told me that it was too soon after the operation. I waited a couple of hours and asked again. She still refused. By this point, I was in a lot of pain. I clicked the buzzer over and over and no one came. After another half hour, Andria saw that I was struggling to hold back tears and knew that it had to be very, very bad for me to be at that point. She went and got the nurse who informed us that there wasn't a doctor on this floor currently and that if she paged him it would take an hour and he would have to leave the ER.

"Excuse me?" I asked. "This is a hospital, there has to be more than one Doctor here."

"Well, I'll go ahead and page him then since you can't seem to wait." She hissed as she walked away.

I couldn't believe this. They just got done drilling six holes in one of my bones and tacking a plate to it and now the healthcare professionals at the Veteran Affairs hospital are getting mad at the veteran for asking them to help manage his pain. Two hours later, the doctor showed up and asked how I was doing.

"Look doc, I know you're busy but this is madness. This pain is smashing me to pieces right now."

"Okay, well I have some good stuff for you here." He replied as he drew a clear drug from a small vile.

"What is that?"

"It's called Ketorolac. It's pretty strong."

"Ketorolac? You're giving me Toradol? That's an NSAID!" I could tell that the Doctor was surprised that I knew what he was administering.

"How about you give me something a little stronger than IV Motrin?" Rather than inquiring as to how I had an intimate knowledge of pharmacology, how I studied it day in and day out and had my own key to a pharmacy for years, he assumed that I was 'a seeker' and must have advised that I not get any narcotics. It was a terribly uncomfortable night to say the least. The throbbing in my shoulder felt like a bass drum sending violent echoes of pain throughout my entire body.

Every time I was able to get a nurse in my room, they would simply roll their eyes at me and tell me that it shouldn't hurt that bad. But it did hurt that bad. For some reason it was one of the most excruciating pains that I have ever experienced and I wasn't being taken seriously. I wasn't seeking drugs, I was seeking comfort. I buzzed for help getting out of bed to use the toilet and waited, and waited. After close to ten minutes, I winced and fought to pull myself out of the tall hospital bed. Using the wall like a crutch I staggered down the hall toward the bathroom. The heavy set nurse behind the desk that I had been trying to ask for help popped up and said,

"You're not supposed to be moving around on your own!"

"Well it was either this or I would have been lying in my own piss for the rest of the day because Lord knows, you weren't going to get off your ass to change those sheets!" She snarled back some bullshit that I had no interest in hearing.

By half-past ten in the morning, my body had already gone through the calories from breakfast and I needed food. At the time of my accident, I was consuming no less than six thousand calories a day because of my high training volume. It wasn't abnormal to have four full meals by noon. I tried asking for something to eat, but was told that I had just eaten and would have to wait until lunchtime. So I called Andria. Within a half hour she swooped in with a very recognizable brown paper bag. My salivary response was immediate as she peeled back the foil that swathed one of the most marvelous creations that has ever been assembled by man. Few things in this world maintain the capacious real estate in my heart as a Chipotle burrito.

Just as I sunk my teeth in for that first glorious bite the nurse entered the room and barked, "You're not supposed to have outside food in here."

I had had enough. That was my breaking point. Despite the intense pain, I stood up, pulled out my own IV line and began walking out of the hospital. The nurses screeched and yelled at me, telling me that I wasn't allowed to leave yet. I told them they should be ashamed to call themselves healthcare providers, and that the veterans in this hospital deserve a lot better treatment than they were willing to provide. That may sound harsh, but I have been in or around the healthcare industry my entire life. My mother was an RN, my father a paramedic, and most of my best friends are PAs or Doctors. Every one of them was appalled at the way patients were treated at the VA.

Every one of my checkups, I was treated like a second rate citizen in a facility that was literally crumbling. I was a terrible obligation, not a patient. This is how our warriors are treated by the very people that are paid to help them. I don't believe that every person working for the VA hospitals across the country is terrible at their job. However, every time I speak with fellow veterans, men whose lives were synonymous with suffering for years without complaint, they seem to express similar concerns about how they themselves have been treated.

I was given enough prescription narcotics to kill a herd of horses. Ninety of this to be filled three times, and sixty of that to be filled three times. I had heard that the VA was liberal with handing out drugs, but this honestly surprised me, especially after being all but denied any painkillers immediately following my surgery. Those who say, "just suck it up." Or, "I don't like to take pain killers even when I'm hurt," don't really understand cellular physiology. When pain receptors are firing like hate being dropped from an AC-130 Gunship, it impedes the healing process of the damaged cells. Pain management is a very important aspect of the healing process. This is another reason I was shocked that I was denied the opportunity to heal appropriately immediately following my operation.

Like many houses in Colorado, ours did not have air conditioning. When we returned from the hospital, I posted up on the couch in our living room and popped a couple of Percocet with a Flexeril and Promethazine, and of course, washed it down with a glass of Jameson. Knowing that the heat was sweltering, my good friends Jess and Anna brought me a small window air conditioning unit, along with enough snacks to help keep my mind off of the situation. I went from being in the best shape of my entire life to a useless, heaping pile of immobile crap on the couch. I was left alone all day with my thoughts, thoughts I had been running from for years.

Every time they began to surface before, I would just go run fifteen miles until I was so exhausted that I couldn't feel those feelings anymore. That was no longer an option. My girlfriend worked a retail job to keep the bills paid and then coached all the classes at the gym in the evening so it wouldn't go under. I sat at home with my friends Ben and Jerry and Jameson, all the while finally being overrun by the suppressed memories of combat. Every detail of the most intense missions played out in front of me as I sat sweating on that grey sofa. If I couldn't run those demons out I was going to put myself under. My cocktail would eventually evolve into two Percocet, two Vicodin, four Flexeril, a Promethazine, and a half a bottle of Jameson every 12 hours or so.

For close to two months, I was useless. My girlfriend would return home more exhausted than the day before. I was failing her. I had told her how this was going to go, how having our own business would change things, and so far all it had meant to her was more work than she ever imagined. Picture walking in the front door after working two jobs, day after day and seeing the person who is supposed to be supporting you higher than two Whitney Houston's and a Charlie Sheen. It's not that it bothered her, it's that it bothered me. I was useless as a provider, as an athlete, and as a human being.

Not being able to physically exhaust myself was becoming a real issue. I believe that exercise is a primary way that most combat veterans deal with their stress. It is something that is very familiar and that we tend to be good at. The chemical release associated with intense physical exertion creates a calming effect. We use it as a form of self-medication, one which we can easily monitor our own dosage. I can't count the number of nights that I ran a sub six-minute mile pace through campus while I was in school. One of many days when a sophomoric 19 year old regurgitated a flippant statement that he heard from one of his professors about 'the real state of Iraq' or how 'We' shouldn't be over there, resulted in one of many sleepless nights trying to run the hate away. Every step I took, I felt like the only human being with these problems. If I wasn't, then why were the streets so empty? I would typically get home with enough time to shower and have a protein shake before the sun came up and I would head to class.

Moving to Colorado would serve to remove me from the hordes of ignorant 19 year olds, yet the skeletons managed to maintain themselves in my closet. The only thing that changed was the triggers that set those bony bastards dancing. Now here I was, one of the only effective coping mechanisms I have ever known, eliminated by a white car and the snapping of a few bones. Besides exercise, alcohol was the only other thing that successfully made me numb. Now I had an almost endless supply of narcotics to act in synergy with that glorious golden solution. This would be my second downward spiral since leaving the military. I was ingesting enough drugs and alcohol in a single day to sedate a horse.

My dreams became lucid. It was apparent that even in a near comatose state, I couldn't escape the reality of my past. The faces were too real. I was not watching my dreams unfold; I was reliving suppressed memories in perfect detail every time I drifted to sleep. I felt the drip of sweat roll down my neck to join the others that had collected underneath my body armor. My faded brown t-shirt had been absorbing the salty moisture for the last three kilometers as we walked to the objective. We had offset infil via pave hawk helicopters, five klicks from the objective. These were not the open fuselage 160th SOAR Blackhawks that we were used to. They were cramped and hot and frequently leaked hydraulic fluid. It's not that any of us minded the three mile walk, especially if it meant a better chance at a firefight when we arrived; we had just been spoiled by having the 160th SOAR drop us at the devil's doorstep each night.

We had been watching the small village that we were now approaching for the last few nights provided by the drones circling overhead. We had watched the TV screen in the command center each evening as two fighting age men left a small house on the outside of the village with weapons in hand to bed down in the fig orchard a few hundred meters away. Our platoon had been in Iraq for about two months and the level of violence that we had been bringing to the area was already known to most. Fighting age males began sleeping outside to avoid being caught in a close quarter combat battle that they knew they could not win. Our platoon had conducted a minimum of one mission per night since arriving in Iraq and kept a running tally of the known terrorists that we had killed and captured.

The primary mission that night was a High Value Target (HVT) in the village. This was a target that could easily be compromised if the two sentries in the field are able to get any shots off. Knowing this, my good friend Allen had his squad mount suppressors to their M4's prior to the start of the mission. As we got closer to the objective a very calm professional silence fell over the group of Rangers. It was time to go to work. The platoon comes to a short halt as the point man draws a pair of tin snips from his pack and cuts away the fence blocking our path. One by one we duck through the obstacle. The green light of my single night vision lens illuminates the path to the enemy.

The way a big cat on the Serengeti crouches and inches closer to its unsuspecting prey, the men of first platoon crept silently through the fig orchard. Each of us wanted to get to those two men first. Each of us wanted their blood on our hands. Killing was our reason for living and the way that every Ranger I have ever known embraces the task at hand none of us were timid about it. I was close, not more than 15 feet away as my heel met the ground first and the outer edge of my foot rolled to meet the soil with meticulous intention, the way my father taught me when hunting javelin in thick brush. Breathing is even; it matches the steps. Heart rate is slightly elevated but calm. I can feel my friend Allen moving a few feet ahead of me. He halts like the lead dog on a hunt. He found them. He had to have. I hear what sounds like a brief rustling of leaves and then *zip zip, zip zip*. I know that sound. That is the sound of a suppressed M4 being discharged in the vast bleak desert air. I rush passed the few trees between Allen and my position with an instant burst that would challenge most world-class sprinters.

I ran into Allen's back and see two men with AK47s laying on their chests with bandoleers hanging from the branch above each of their collapsed heads. One of the men's eyes was hanging out as the 5.56 round had impacted just right to create enough pressure to pop it like a zit. Brains cover Allen's light brown desert combat boot, a fact that didn't seem to concern him. The platoon sergeant was there within another breath. "What the fuck?! I told you to wait…. I wanted one of those fuckers!"

Allen just shrugged the way a teenager does after missing curfew by 5 minutes. "I'm just kidding, good job Allen." Apparently one of the men opened his eyes as Allen was standing over him. Seeing Allen, who was intimidating as hell wearing body armor with an assault rifle pointed at his head caused the insurgent to reach for his weapon. That was enough for Allen to play matchmaker between him and all those virgins he was promised. A few minutes later the "combat" cameraman makes his way to the scene with all the stealth and grace of a herd of buffalo. He seemed upset that we hadn't waited for him. Zero fucks were given.

We began to make our way out of the orchard and into the town. The hot water from my camelback passed through the tube and into my mouth as we pushed toward the HVT's house in the village. After so many nights of doing this, my aid bag had become a part of my body; I didn't even notice its weight on my shoulders anymore. 2nd Squad was taking the lead on the target house just ahead of us. I'm not sure if I had become so used to the radio chatter that I didn't hear it or there was none, but it seemed silent as we all instinctively fell into our positions before entering the house.

The image of the man's eye dangling from the side of his collapsed skull flashed before me as I enter the first house. There was already a couple of Rangers ahead of me. I heard shots ring out from the back of the back of the house. I was not responsible to any specific fire team or squad, giving me the ability to forgo clearing the tertiary rooms and adjacent houses and head right for the throat of the fight. My need to be at the center of chaos didn't always sit well with the men that I was tasked to fix in the event of them being injured.

A woman laid screaming in bed as I entered the sticky, hot room; her husband's insides covering the bed and the dresser. In the room next door an infant is whaling. The man, still half asleep, made a move for a nearby pistol and met his fate the same way as his two counterparts in the field. The child's crying grew louder and louder, its sound morphs to a high pitch buzzing.

I felt the sweat roll from my hairline into my eye and am snapped awake. I found myself laying on the floor ten feet away from the grey couch that I had passed out on several hours ago and noticed the TV was on but has converted to the *This concludes the broadcast day-screen*.

I looked around in a panic and was relieved to find the large bottle of pills and a quarter bottle of Jameson left on the coffee table. I groaned in pain as I rolled toward my only comfort, my right arm still immobilized by the sling protecting my freshly repaired collarbone. I attempted to blink away the image of the man sliced open in bed next to his wife along with the two men in the field. Normally, I would head immediately to my running shoes. I couldn't even tie them by myself if I wanted to let alone go for a run. My outstretched hand found the bottle and I began to self-medicate the only other way I knew how.

No matter how much my girlfriend did, she would never understand those moments. She was the only one there yet it didn't seem to matter at all. I felt like the only person to have ever gone through these things and because of this I refused to tell anyone about them. No one would understand, how could they? The other men that went through the same type of events on the same nights weren't having an issue dealing with any of this, or so I thought. So why was I? Was I that weak that I couldn't handle the killing of several dozen people? It wasn't difficult at the time, why was it weighing on me now?

Chapter 14: Bury Your Flame

With time, the physical wounds began to fuse. The filthy torment of crepitus from broken bones was becoming a memory while the fragmented memories of the past seemed to be coagulating into a much more complete story line. Physically, I wasn't ready to return to work but I had no choice. I would not be able to survive another week on that couch. The tolerance that I had established for painkillers was impressive; thankfully the VA gave me plenty. There was no mention of physical therapy or follow up appointments, just a lot of pills to keep me sedated.

The same week that I found the strength to leave the living room, we were informed that we were being evicted from our house. It wasn't for a lack of payment but rather the woman who had owned the home had just passed away and willed the home to her 17-year-old niece. The girl's parents decided that they had no interest in being landlords and told us that we had until the end of the month to be out.

Insult meet injury.

We didn't have the time or money to move and I would have been very little help in the condition that I was in. We pleaded our case to the new homeowners but they politely refused our request for an extension. I had no control over anything at this point. I was failing everything. My entire life I refused to ask for help and I wasn't going to start now, despite how utterly bleak the situation was. The copious amount of pride that I had would be no match for my Ranger buddies, however.

I must have told them a dozen times not to worry about it, but on the day that it came to move Jess and his wife, Anna, were both at my front door. It wasn't the first time that they had stepped up for me and it wouldn't be the last. It has taken me years to realize that helping a brother in need isn't just about the one that needs help. Every time, I have had the opportunity to do a tiny bit of good in the lives of my Ranger buddies, I have jumped at the opportunity. We spent years propping each other up through hard times. Those actions give an indescribably sense of self-worth and necessity. I needed to exist because my brothers depended on me every day! When that disappears so goes with it your sense of self-worth. I have the greatest group of friends that any human being can have. It has taken me a very long time to understand that not asking them for help when I truly need it is just as detrimental to them as it is to me. Swallowing my pride enables others to reclaim their once unparalleled value.

We moved into a tiny apartment close to the gym and close to Jess and Anna. Along with my good friend and fellow Ranger, Nathan, they would insure that I would not fall through the cracks. I decided one day that I had to drop the pills. They had their hooks in me too deep. I still had some left but I had to regain some sort of control. Just like that I stopped. The cold sweats and vomiting were unexpected but only lasted a couple of days. I owed it to the men that never came back to be more than a junkie. They didn't get the choice how to spend their late twenties and I wasn't going to dishonor them by wasting mine.

I told myself that as soon as my hand could reach the handlebar of my bike that I would be back in the saddle. I drew heavily on my time in Ranger Battalion during that time. I had bounced back from surgeries before, this would be no different. I bounced back from that and I was going to bounce back from this.

Twelve hours after the first time that my right shoulder had sufficient mobility to lift and extend my arm to reach the shifting lever of my Specialized Tarmac, I headed out. With a group of friends riding all around me, I headed directly for the spot that I was knocked off my bike a few weeks before. As we approached the seemingly unassuming patch of asphalt, I felt my anxiety rise. My heart elevated well beyond the 80 rotations my pedals were making each minute. I could hear my breathing for the first time during the ride. 100 meters away. The cars are zipping by. 50 meters. The wind gusts. 20 meters. POP!!!!!

The uneven death grip on my handlebars causes them to shake and I nearly veered into the same soft dirt that ruined my last bike jersey. My friend, Mike

Lavera's inner tube exploded at what must have been the absolute worst time in history of blowouts. We quickly pulled off to the side and repaired it without incident, and by the end of the 40-mile ride, I knew that the pills were in my past and that I was mentally stronger than this injury. What I didn't realize at the time, however, was that I was trading one addiction for another. Sure I wasn't popping pills for relief anymore, but I also wasn't actually doing anything to fix the root problem.

If the incident had one silver lining, it was that it showed me that if things go bad, I could rely on Andria. Knowing that someone would be there when things got difficult is such an integral part of a relationship. I was accustomed to having people in my life that would not abandon me regardless of how tumultuous things got. As unfair as it may seem, I held her and every other women in my life to the same standard that had been set by my brothers in arms.

They were all willing to fight to the death for me so it shouldn't be too much to ask of her, right?

I believe that this subconscious expectation is one that acts detrimentally to many relationships in the lives of combat veterans. It takes an incredibly strong and confident woman to handle a personality like ours. The expectation to be readily adaptable to any and all situations somehow ends up carrying over from the military into our relationships. There is an expectation of undying loyalty, courage and above all else, an ability to read a map on a road trip. I'm not saying that is fair, it's just the way it tends to be.

When I was young, I watched my mother completely destroy my father. She took from him everything that he had, and I always vowed to not repeat his mistake. I told myself that I would never give enough of myself to anyone that had the capacity to destroy me. Yet somehow when Andria stood by me during such tribulation it made me believe that this would be different, that I could step out of that mindset. She already had my love but now she had my trust. I already knew that she was good on road trips and now knew I could count on her when things got tough. On the morning of her birthday, as the sun crested through the space between the drapes in our bedroom, I asked her to marry me, giving her a modest ring and a promise that I would always be there for her the way that she was there for me. I had a bottle of Champagne hidden in the refrigerator and we shared a few mimosas before having to open the business.

Her happiness seemed to overflow. It was genuine and it was something that I created and that felt amazing. I gladly coached every class while she called everyone that she knew. She was truly radiating with joy. It solidified to me that it was the right choice and I began to imagine what being a husband would look like. My mind's eye painted a picture of the story of our future together, our wedding, our first child being born, and how even into our later years we would continue our adventures around the world together.

Life is an amazing mystery. We want so badly to move swiftly forward but while still chained to the weights of our past, we are racing futility. As it often does, summer shifted to fall and the leaves of love and joy gradually morphed to a darker shade. They fell from our tree not at once but slowly, methodically, and without notice.

The financial strain associated with starting a business was significant. Add to that the weight of emotionally suppressing the tenebrous memories of combat, and a twisted screeching demon that could only be silenced with alcohol arose once more. No amount of love could seem to combat the dreams, guilt, and feelings of isolation that dominated my life. Having to work 80-90 hours every week in an effort to maintain a successful business placed an even greater strain on our relationship. Neither of us had a day off in months.

When things fall apart, they seldom do so neatly; rather the way an old star's existence comes to an end, so goes the hot flame of desire. There were disagreements but that comes with any relationship. Things piled up and instead of dealing with them, we ignored them. The beginning of the end echoed the intensity of my life. It was extreme, but extreme had always been my norm. I loved her like I've never loved anyone but love is just as vulnerable to the caustic effects of madness as anything else. I expected her to understand the war I was fighting in my head without sharing any of it with her.

I didn't know how to communicate my struggles with her because I didn't understand them myself. I didn't know why I had to train so much or why I drank so much. In my own mind, the only thing that was out of line was how she responded to me. She was overreacting to things that, to me, seemed normal. I placed her on the same level with the men that I served with because I trusted her the way that I trusted them. The problem was she didn't have the same ability to comprehend my struggles the way that Matt did when I returned from those college classes so upset. She couldn't have just known yet somehow I expected her to. Trust and communication are the two most important aspects of a relationship and we had been operating at fifty percent for too long.

Nearly a year had gone by since my accident and despite a few lingering pains, I was back to racing. The process of laying out all of my gear the night before a race mimicked my ritual in Iraq. *Helmet?* Check. *Water bottles?* Check. *Skittles*? Check. *Eight 30 round mags of 5.56*? Don't think that is going to fit in my kit this time.

The process was so comforting to me that I would do it multiple times. There was a very specific timeline to this ritual, just as there was for a combat mission. There was a series of tasks that needed to be accomplished in a very specific order to ensure the overall success of the operation. If bike tires are inflated too soon, they lose pressure and create greater rolling resistance causing a slower bike time. If the batteries in your radio are changed out and turned on too soon, you risk having it die in the middle of a mission. As a result, this ritual became very important to me. Racing was my substitute for combat and the hours leading up to it were crucial.

One of the most important aspects of the pre-race timeline is when and what an athlete eats. A couple of years prior, while doing my first half Ironman race, I had very few options as to what I could eat. Jimmy Johns was pretty much it so I ordered two number 12s (which I found out later is vastly inferior to "The Gold Coast" at Fat Jack's). I did very well at that race and so I made sure to always eat that same sandwich the night before racing.

I had offered to cover the Friday night hours at the gym for Andria while I did my layouts in the office. She asked if she could help in anyway so I asked if she could pick up my sandwiches. She agreed and told me she would be right back. The Jimmy Johns was only about a mile from the gym. An hour later I locked up for the night assuming that she must be meeting me at home. To my surprise she wasn't there when I returned. I was instantly worried so I called her cell phone. She told me that she had run into a couple of friend's downtown and would be home soon. Okay, she was alright, which was a relief. It's getting past the point where I should eat though and this could affect things if she doesn't show up soon. I waited and waited. Several hours later, at around midnight she stumbled through the front door drunk.

I didn't respond well to that. I'm not saying that what she did was okay; however, looking back now I know I could have responded with more maturity. She should have been more important to me than the race. This wasn't about a race though. To her it was. To me this was a mission that was just compromised by her negligent apathy. I didn't have the ability to differentiate between the two. I didn't want to. Although I didn't know it at the time, I needed something in my life to replace the cadence of combat. I needed something to be that important again.

Chapter 15: A Letter

The vitriol between us increased, as antagonistic text messages volleyed back and forth like gunshots, each one causing more damage than the one before. Every day was another escalation of force until we reached cataclysm. She had moved in with a friend leaving me alone with my vices.

I tried for a brief moment to reason with her when she showed up with a friend to gather the remainder of her belongings from our home. She wasn't interested in that conversation. I couldn't sit there and watch my life walk out the door. So I did what I do. I went to a patio bar and drank enough IPA to sink a ship before the sun went down. I met a random group of people that invited me back to their house for a BBQ. We continued to take shots of Jack Daniels until I found myself in the back bedroom with two of the women at the party.

They had both been flirting with me for hours. Since Andria and I first met, I hadn't noticed another woman in a sexual way. There was no desire in me for anyone else. The thought of her packing her things at this moment broke my heart. I was lost. I was hurt and I didn't just hate her for what she was doing to me, I hated all women. No broken bone or tearing of flesh had ever caused me the kind of pain I was experiencing in that moment. I refused to hold the weight of that torment alone.

I fucked them both in some stranger's house. My typical assertive nature in the bedroom seemed to be amplified by the situation. With her legs wrapped around my waist, I slammed the brunette into the wall with such force that it left a massive hole in the drywall, all the while the taller blonde laid and watched. She would be next. The combination of whiskey and rage fueled the next two straight hours of sweaty, unwavering lust. It seemed as though nothing was off limits as I took every bit of frustration and anger and fear out on them. Without so much as asking either of their names, I recovered my pants, shirt and the only one of my socks that I could find, and headed back to a completely empty apartment.

Everything was gone. After all of the laughter and love, the joy and the pain, our existence together was over. She had moved on and I was left in an empty apartment to absorb the mistakes of my own character. The fallout from that incident left me staring at a blank wall that was once covered with pictures of the two of us. She would later tell me that my obsession with racing combined with my tendency to overreact was what caused her to leave. I told her that I would never do another triathlon again if that is what it took to get her back but I don't think it would have helped even if she had agreed. The fallout from the separation would result in my third, and most catastrophic, downward spiral.

Things were bad, then they were worse. She came into the gym in the middle of the night and took most of the office, including all of the writing utensils and members' liability waivers. She took thousands of dollars of equipment when no one was there because she felt entitled to it. I was left running a two person business by myself without the funds to do it. Right around this time, most of the money in the business checking account came up missing leaving me the captain of a sinking ship. The only thing that remained as anything resembling common ground was my dog, Jameson. She had fallen in love with that dopey mutt over the last two years. Early on in the breakup, I agreed that she could take Jameson overnight once a week as long as I got her back.

One day she decided not to bring her back. I called and sent emails and text messages but got no response. Two more days went by and I threatened to call the police. I found out through a mutual friend that she was in the process of getting new shots and registering Jameson in her name. I called the sheriff's office and animal control, both of which told me there was nothing I could do. I filed a police report with the city but they told me it was somehow a county issue. This wasn't a set of pots and pans I was losing, it wasn't some kettlebells and yoga mats, hell it wasn't even a dog, this was friend. She had been there for me when I returned from Iraq and had gladly traversed back and forth across the country with me for years before my girlfriend and I had ever met. The overwhelming, misplaced sense of entitlement that it takes to kidnap a living creature is disturbing to me. I had no clue where she was living and her friends certainly were not talking.

Due to the fact that so many people left the gym in the wake of the drama associated with our separation, I could no longer pay my bills. I was living on the discounted bread from the bakery section and hadn't been able to pay my phone or credit card bills in months. I only had a few more days before I would be forced out of my apartment. I had already sold several things in an effort to make ends meet but it wasn't enough. I had been working close to 90 hours a week for over three months trying to keep my business from closing and I couldn't even afford to pay the $615 rent on my tiny apartment.

My world had collapsed. Everything that was once good was now in flames and I still hadn't done a damn thing to address the demons that had for years been taunting my sanity. I was beyond exhausted. I was defeated and alone. In the sweltering summer heat of a place where I couldn't afford air conditions, I went to the medicine cabinet where the smorgasbord of pill bottles provided by the VA had been sitting for a year. I didn't want to be alive another minute. This is where they would find me whoever *they* would be; maybe the maintenance man responding to a complaint of a foul odor would discover me. Perhaps the rental office trying to get a very late rent check. I Googled the lethal dosage for each. I had already been drinking heavily and counted out the appropriate number.

I organized the pills and thought of nothing at all. It was a truly unexpected calm that settled over me in that moment. Reaching for the fistful of end game, my phone buzzed, a text message from one of my oldest and dearest friends back in Phoenix. He had served as a Marine Sergeant and was a man that I hold in the highest regard. His message was completely out of the blue, a hundred percent random.

"Hey brother, I know it's been months since we've spoken but I just wanted to say how much I respect you and how much of an inspiration you have always been. Your strength is real, brother."

My right fist was clenching the narcotics, my left fist was clenching hope and the muscles of my face were clenching, trying to hold back the tears that were obstructing the vision of my bloodshot eyes. An obnoxious light interrupted the perfect calm darkness of my world. A glimmer of sanguinity.

The seemingly simple act of randomly reaching out to his friend and fellow veteran literally saved my life. It is all too easy of a thing to do and can make all the difference in the world yet is something that we just don't do enough. We are a very prideful, stubborn bunch and most likely are not going to ask for help when we need it most. I needed help in that moment but refused to ask for it. That message caused me to swallow my pride instead of those pills and I am forever grateful to you for that, Mark, my friend, my brother.

Looking at the situation I realized that it was completely unsustainable. There was absolutely no way

I could keep the gym open and survive. Despite the massive amount of emotional support I was receiving from my friends and gym members I would be forced to make one of the most difficult decisions of my entire life. I had to close my business. I had to let down a group of people that believed in me. I had to look them in the face and tell them that I wasn't going to be able to help them anymore. I was retreating and that didn't sit well with me. My father insisted to me that it wasn't retreating; rather I was regrouping for an even greater assault forward.

A couple of weeks before my 29th birthday my business closed. I was unemployed and forced to leave my shitty one bedroom apartment. Jess and Anna, friends that were already more like family, insisted that I stay with them until I found a new place. Despite how well they knew me, I am not quite sure they knew what they were inviting into their home at this time. I was out of the bottom of the abyss, but I was no way on top of a mountain. The way I saw it, I had nothing. In reality, I had the only thing that matters. I had a group of people that loved and supported me despite having nothing. I now know how easy it is for people to be behind you when you are on top of your game, when you have everything that you need. It is a complete other thing when people prop you up when you have nothing to give in return.

For the next few weeks, I sat on their couch watching Madmen in my underwear and going drink for drink with Donald Draper. Most wives would tolerate this behavior from their husband's friends for about a day before stepping in, not a Ranger wife, not Anna. She would return from a hard day's work and find Jess and I drinking beers, watching Transformers like a couple of teenagers. Instead of getting mad, she would order us pizza and crack open a beer. She drew the line when Jess and I decided to split a hundred chicken McNuggets. She didn't try to stop us; she just shook her head in disgust as we challenged our bodies to digest the food-like substance. I wasn't sober much during that time, but I never felt like I was being judged. Once or twice I heard, "Leo, don't you have an Ironman coming up in a week or two? Maybe you should go train for that."

They were right. I had an Ironman race coming up and hadn't done much in the way of preparing. It was difficult to tell if I cared at all about the race or if I was hiding on my bike the same way that I hid in the bottle. I had no intention in confronting my demons and no interest in debriding the wounds that were clearly becoming infected. Once again, I drowned my sorrows in mile repeats on the track, tall glasses of whiskey, long mountain bike rides, and copious amounts of beer. My 6th place overall was my best finish at that distance yet did little to improve my outlook on things.

I needed to get out of Colorado. Everywhere I looked reminded me of some failure or another. I made plans to retreat back home to Phoenix. I had been accepted into an exercise physiology program at Northern Arizona University and was excited to put every bit of the past few months in my rear view mirror. I reserved the U Haul trailer for Tuesday afternoon and went to have a few beers with Jess on Sunday night. Little did I know that I would be in jail when I was supposed to be picking up that trailer.

Chapter 16: To Withstand the Force of Storms

Since the very first day of basic training, Jess had been one of my best friends. We suffered a lot of moments together during and after the military. That history together allowed each of us to feel the other's pain. Knowing that we wouldn't be seeing each other for a while, the two of us decided to share a few beers in downtown Golden, Colorado at a bar called Ace High. When Anna came to pick us up several hours later we were both a little south of sober. I was told later that I jumped from the moving car in an effort to chase down two deer. Apparently I got pretty close too.

I woke up the next morning in bed cuddled up to Jameson. Not the bottle, my dog. With only one eye open, I attempted to assess the situation. The next sound I heard was a pounding on the door and a voice I was all too familiar with. That was the voice of my very pissed off ex. Anna answered the door. All I really heard from the exchange was Anna saying, "It's not your fucking dog!" I had to smile. I already had three sisters but I'll be damned if Anna hadn't earned her place as number four! She always had my back.

Half of an hour later there was another knock, this one was much more aggressive and was followed with the tag-line no hung-over person wants to hear, "Golden Police Department, open up!" Well, that escalated quickly. There are two things I don't like, when people brush their teeth in front of me, and being incarcerated. So I just kind of hung out with the dog and let someone else answer the door. Jess and Anna did their best to explain the situation to the officer but he wanted to hear it from me. In hindsight, I should have shimmied down the drainpipe and fled to the Subway down the street for a delicious breakfast sandwich.

Instead, I peeled myself from my sheets and headed out the door to talk to the officer. The officer immediately appeared on guard which was odd considering I was barely capable of keeping one half of one eye open in my condition. Apparently my ex had told him that I was crazy and had PTSD from Iraq. She told him that I was a Ranger and that I worked for Blackwater and that I was very unstable. I was able to hear the original 911 call a couple of months later, along with the reading the police report, you would think I was John Rambo.

I made pleasant with the gentlemen while propping myself up against a rail.

I asked him if he would kindly remove his hand from his side arm as it made me pretty uncomfortable. He just said, "No."

Okay, I can see how this is going to go, I am the abusive boyfriend no matter what I say. She had spent the last twenty minutes playing up the, I'm just a defenseless girl, she used the, *I'm a victim card* with terrifying precision and I could tell that he had already bought it hook line and sinker.

I tried joking with him and his partner, asking them if either had a Tylenol in an effort to show that I wasn't a threat. It didn't help. I explained the backstory and that the dog they were inquiring about had been mine for years before we even met. I calmly responded to her allegations that I 'stole the dog' with the fact that you can't steal something that was already yours. It was my dog.

At this point, there was no confirmation that I even had the dog in my possession. I explained how utterly silly the entire thing was. I asked why when I called the exact same department to file a report about my dog being stolen, they told me that there was nothing that they could do. Now I am standing here trying to explain myself to a police officer, one that is treating me like a dangerous criminal, for allegedly stealing something that already belonged to me. He asked me if the dog was inside. I informed him that it doesn't matter where my dog is, *it's my dog.* Once again my hindsight is 20/20. Looking back I should have lied to the man when he asked again if my dog was inside the apartment. I should have told him to go get a warrant and find out, go get a warrant for a missing dog.

Unfortunately for me, I felt compelled to explain. I know better now. I had told the officer that I was feeling restless the night before and went for a run, something that I did on a very regular basis. He didn't believe me. "Oh, I'm supposed to believe that crap?" He asked in a condescending tone. "You just went for a stroll in the middle of the night and ended up miles away?"

I informed him that I had just come in 6th place overall in an Ironman and going for a three mile stroll wasn't really that absurd of a concept. I continued to tell him that I saw a dog that looked familiar in the street and realized it was Jameson. I then carried her home and woke up the next day to a knocking on the door.

Jess informed him that he was also a law enforcement officer. He corroborated my story but was told by the officer that, "If I want your opinion on my investigation I will tell you, now go sit down."

I couldn't believe the disrespect this person was displaying. He asked one more time if the dog was inside the apartment. I finally told him yes, my dog is inside my home. "Okay, put your hands behind your back." The officer recited.

"For what!? I didn't break any laws. I haven't done anything illegal." He wouldn't explain why, he just repeated his demand, this time in a more aggressive tone almost trying to incite me. This guy was prodding me because he had a badge.

He knew I have served multiple combat deployments as a Ranger and has chosen this entire time to speak to me without a fragment of respect. He wants to put those cuffs on me and take away my freedom, a freedom that I have already killed to preserve. This is the society that my friends died for. We live in a time and place where we glorify military service upon entry and vilify it upon separation. We live in a society that would rather fear its veterans than attempt to actually understand them. War fighters get an occasional pat on the head but for the most part the society that we fight for has no real interest in our plight. To those that haven't fought for it, freedom seems to be little more than a talking point.

Some people may say that the officer was simply doing his job. I understand that perspective but I do not share it. I never had a reason to mistrust police before this moment. I grew up in a fire station where officers would frequently stop in for lunch. When I was a firefighter in Arizona we worked with DPS and local Sheriffs on a daily basis. I was discriminated against because I was a war veteran. To him I was dangerous because of what I had done in the past.

I knew I didn't have to go to jail right then. I knew with 100% certainty that I had the ability to rip that man apart. Instead, I calmly placed my hands behind my back and took in the last free breath I was going to get for a while. Combat veterans are like pit bulls, we get a bad rap for mauling people every now and then but that only happens following a great deal of abuse. There is a negative stigma attached to the bread because we have an aggressive appearance. Those that fear us do so because they are ignorant and simply follow what they have heard others say. One 30 second news story about a pit bull attacking a person or a veteran with post traumatic stress undermines the millions of friendly, loyal, caring majority. Let's be honest though, telling a story about a disabled combat vet working day in and day out without incident to support his family isn't exactly "newsworthy.

I sat handcuffed in the back of a patrol car and watched as the officer went into the apartment, retrieved my therapy dog, my friend, and handed her over to my ex. I was charged with felony burglary, trespassing and domestic violence. She had told the officer that I had broken into her house in the middle of the night and stole the dog, her dog. I offered to show the officer all of the shot records and adoption paperwork that predated the start of our relationship, but he said it didn't matter. She cried and sold a story about an abusive, dangerous vet and he ate it up with zero evidence to suggest there was any truth at all to her story.

The naked concrete in my holding cell was frigid and unavoidable. I figured that I would be out in an hour or two given the nonsense nature of the charges. Instead, I was told that I was being transferred to the county jail where I would be processed and kept until I could be seen by a judge. I was transported to Jefferson County Jail late in the afternoon. I was made to strip down, surrender my clothes and don something similar to the scrubs that I had worn while performing trauma surgeries during the Special Operations Medical Course a few years before. I was placed in a holding cell with about a dozen other guys who all seemed more familiar with this environment than I did. I wasn't really scared or intimidated. I knew if anyone tried anything that I could completely handle myself. I was more concerned with the legal repercussions of such an event. If someone attacked me, I would not hesitate to use the full force of my capability to defend myself. That could easily mean killing a man. A violent offence added to the list of charges that got me here would solidify any case brought against me.

We sat and waited to be brought to our cells. The experience felt very similar to when I in-processed on day one of the Army. The overly assertive gentlemen hollering commands, the group of like-dressed men standing in a file, not allowed to look left or right, the primary concern being when we would be fed being silently echoed by the entire group. To my surprise, I was brought to the maximum-security floor. *For dog-napping? Really?* I was placed in my own cell that was about 8'x10'. It had a steal sink, toilet without a seat, and two mattresses. There was a small window in the back of the cage that I approached and peered through for as long as the sun still hung in the sky. I laughed to myself thinking of someday in the future where I would have the opportunity to start a story with, "You ever watch the sun set over the Rockies… from a jail cell?" Sure it wasn't a joyous experience but it was a life experience nonetheless. I was living something that most people never will and as a result I was growing as a human being.

Life is a big game filled with sorrow and solace alike. There is no surviving it, you won't make it out alive but there is a way to win. Embrace and evolve. The waves of life will never stop crashing at your shore. Fighting will leave you weary and woeful. Learn to surf. Take advantage of life's adversity to expand yourself, to become a better version of yourself each and every day. Despite my contempt for being in this situation I was still going to learn from it.

When the guard slid the plastic tray of "food" through the slot in the six inch thick door I had to chuckle. Succotash.... Again. This plate of what looked like turkey, gravy, succotash and some kind of pink cake bore a striking resemblance to every single meal I ever ate in Afghanistan and Iraq. I was hungry but I wasn't that hungry. When the guard came back a few minutes later to collect the tray most of its contents had barely been picked through. I resigned to get some sleep. I tucked myself under the itchy green blanket that once again was reminiscent of the ones we had in the army. At some point in the middle of the night, the door swung open and another inmate was placed into the cell. Well, this is interesting I thought. Looks like I have a roommate. No, wait, I have a cellmate. Wow, I never thought I would have a cellmate. I wonder what he did to get in here. I wonder what he thinks I did to get in here.

He had that "trying to play it cool" look plastered all over his scarred white face. I stood up and took one of the two thin mattresses I had been sleeping on and pulled it to the floor. "There ya go, bud." He looked incredibly relieved that he wasn't going to have to fight me. We didn't say anything to each other. Early the next morning, before the sun came up, another guard came and told me that I was being transferred to Gen Pop. I would learn that was short for general population. Apparently this is supposed to be a better situation than the tiny cell that I was currently occupying, but to be honest, I was more than happy to risk it in here with Slim Shady than be tossed into the mix with 50 criminals. The choice, however, was not mine to make. I no longer had a say in where I went, or what I did or how long I did it for. I was no longer a free man. My freedom, the aspect of humanity that I have always held paramount, had been taken from me.

Arriving in Gen Pop was an experience. It felt like I was in a movie. Guys covered in prison style tattoos were doing pushups and pull-ups in the yard area. Other guys were playing card games to pass the time. I was brought to my bunk and shown my locker. I could tell that I was being sized up in a big way. Every movement that I made was important. I had to act like I had been through this drill a dozen times. *Fake it till you make it,* I thought. It was the same in the military.

I was shown the proper way to make my bed and maintain my belongings. I was told that I was allowed a specific number of personal effects such as books and I would have the opportunity to purchase things like actual shoes. *Holy shit, this was just like the Army!* I settled in and realized that most of this was just about finding ways to kill time. It wasn't really a punishment; it was more like a purgatory. When meals came, I became instantly popular because I refused to eat the desert. I just gave it away. Guys that had been there for a while were shocked by this action. That awful piece of cake was the highlight of their entire day and I didn't care about it at all.

The guy that I shared a bunk bed with had been arrested for the third time. He had stolen a car while on meth. The guy across from my bed was a drug dealer that had been arrested multiple times. Why was I in here with these guys? I still couldn't figure this out. It was as if someone stole my car and I saw it parked in someone else's driveway as I walked by, still having the keys in my pocket, I got in, and drove it home. The car thief called the cops on me though and now I'm in jail; now I was sharing domicile with some pretty world-class bad decision makers.

I finally got my time in front of a judge. Once again Jess and Anna were there to speak on my behalf. The prosecutor tried to say that I was a flight risk because I didn't have a job and shouldn't be released on bail. Having Jess, an officer of the law, give his personal guarantee that he would take full responsibility for me was the only thing that got me released. The following day, I was set free on bond. I would have to check in with my parole officer twice a week and was not allowed to leave the area without getting direct written permission. I was out but I wasn't free. I wasn't allowed to have any type of weapon or alcohol in the house. Jess had to take his firearms to work and leave them there. I felt like the worst friend imaginable. I would have already been to Arizona by the time I got out. Fate had a different plan for me, though.

It is always amusing to me when people tell me about their life plans. Life doesn't give a shit what your plan is, life does what it wants. You are a sock in the spin cycle my friend, your only option is to take the bumps and react. Sure you need to be proactive rather than reactive, but like Tyson said, "everyone has a plan until they get punched in the face." I had a great plan laid out and I just took one huge overhand right from life. I was still standing though. I had no job, no home, no money, no purpose and very little freedom, but I was still standing. The very next day I received a completely random phone call from a good friend that I hadn't spoken with in a while. He wanted to have coffee and run something by me. Little did I know at the time that that call would essentially change just about every aspect of my life.

Chapter 17: First Reactions After Falling Through Ice

I hadn't known Josh as long as many of my other friends. We were not in the military together and he had just recently moved to Colorado. He had been a good friend with one of the athletes at my gym who I respected a great deal. Our mutual friend had brought Josh into my gym to train a few times. When I found out that he was a certified trainer and former professional baseball player, I asked if he would be interested in coaching. Josh in no way needed the money. I think he saw it as a way to help me out. In fact, I actually tried to pay him a few times and he refused.

We had discussed opening a second gym together and even looked at a few locations in Denver. When the drama with my ex and I was going on, the idea of that deal slipped away. I didn't blame Josh or anyone else that created distance with the utter nonsense that was going on during that time. I wish I could have distanced myself from it, too.

Sitting at a coffee shop in downtown Denver, hearing a job offer from Josh was kind of funny to me. A few months ago, I was in a position to give him a job and now the tables had completely turned. He had become partners with an existing gym in Denver and had plans to open another in the coming weeks. They wanted me to come on board and run the endurance programming as well as coach as many classes as I wanted. The gesture itself was incredible to me. Seeing as how I had pretty much been doing that job for free for well over a year, the thought of getting paid was refreshing. I agreed immediately and began looking for an apartment near downtown. I still had the weight of a series of felony charges hanging over my head, but at least now I had a job. In that, I had a glimmer of hope for survival.

Finding a home was an interesting challenge. I wanted to live near the gym where I would be coaching but those places were expensive and went fast. I sat on Craigslist hitting refresh every three minutes. I found a spot that would be perfect that was actually within my meager budget. I called within minutes of the ad going up and told the guy on the other line that I could be there in less than 30 minutes. By the time I got there, he had received 15 other calls. It was a "garden level" which pretty much means that it was a basement that someone converted into an apartment.

I told him that I would take it right now. I was told that he had several other people coming to look at it. He told me that it used to act as an office space for his business but since his ex-fiancé left him, he would have to rent it out. *Oh your fiancé just left huh?*

"Yeah and she is taking the dog that we had together too."

After he heard my story he called the other perspective renters and told them the place was taken. He and I drank many beers together over the next year. I was two for two. I now had a job and a home. I was on the upswing. I had also just been accepted into an exercise physiology program at MSU in Denver. I knew that I had already passed many of the classes required for the major during my time in the military. I had enough time remaining in my Montgomery GI Bill benefits to complete this degree as long as my classes were accepted. I submitted all of my transcripts from the military, an amount totaling ninety-six credits worth of anatomy, physiology, pathophysiology, kinesiology and every other 'ology' there is. Along with all of the liberal arts classes I had taken in Indiana, I would only be responsible for the core degree classes such as exercise physiology, comparative fitness programming and other specific classes.

When I got the transcript report back and saw the "0" next to credits given for military service, I was a little confused. When I say confused, what I mean is, I was pissed! Immediately, I gathered all of my transcripts and course content from all of the schools that I had attended, schools taught by medical doctors with attrition rates higher than just about any medical school in the world. I did what any good Ranger would do; I prepared for a fight. The problem is these fights can't be fought with violence of action. You have to be patient when dealing with people in bureaucratic positions. Their war is a war of stagnation and they fight it every day. This is a lesson that I have had to learn the hard way.

Coming from Special Operations, there is a very high expectation for things to get done and get done the right way the first time. I figured that there had been some mistake made and I would have to wait for weeks or months for the issue to be corrected. It may not be the same in the rest of the military but I can speak for the guys in charge of handling these types of things in Ranger Battalion (the S-1 shop or PAC office), and they are incredibly efficient. If you have an issue with pay or leave or anything that requires paperwork, those guys had it handled before the end of the day.

I sat patiently at the transcript office waiting to inform them of the minor error that they had made. File folder in hand, I was led through a series of cubicles to the one belonging to a woman named Lynn. As politely as I could, I explained that I had submitted my transcripts for evaluation and by some mistake was given zero credit for the classes that I had already demonstrated proficiency in. She looked at the paperwork that I provided to her and just said, "Nope, no mistake. That's not a real school so we won't accept it."

These moments are important. These moments are a type of barometer for how well I have done to assimilate. Initially the reaction to a comment like this, isn't a choice, it's just a reaction. In combat and in the military as a whole you are taught to respond to aggression with more aggression. You are taught escalation of force and violence of action solves problems.

Now I had a very overweight, middle-aged woman telling me that the most comprehensive emergency medical school in the entire world, taught by some of the best paramedics and doctors in the world, wasn't a "real school." Funny, it felt pretty real sitting in class forty hours a week for months on end. It felt real doing the most advanced live tissue training available anywhere. The twenty extra hours a week out of class spent in the cadaver lab drilling anatomy seemed real to me. It felt pretty real scrubbing in and assisting a dozen surgeries, delivering babies, casting arms, stitching lacerations, placing chest tubes, performing surgical cricothyroidotomies, and diagnosing hundreds of sick patients. It felt real watching over 80% of the class fail out or recycle. It felt pretty real graduating shoulder to shoulder with the best trauma medics the world has ever seen, and it sure as shit felt real applying every one of those skills on my friends in shitty third world countries.

Zero. That is the value that this overgrown community college places on all of that. I fully understand that many people will say to just let it slide, that it isn't worth the argument. The issue wasn't with the thought of having to retake every one of the classes that I had already passed, that wouldn't be a problem because I could coast through them. The issue was that this woman, this school, and this society completely undervalue the knowledge and experience of military veterans. That woman could have literally spit in my face and it wouldn't have offended me as much as telling me that SOCM isn't a real school. It was infuriating that she didn't even consider her comments offensive.

Luckily this was not my first encounter of this kind. I had been dealing with ignorant freedom leeches for years now. I decided to swallow the rage that had formed in my belly and had been working its way to my vocal cords. I asked her to look at specific courses in the degree that I was pursuing, one of which being first aid and CPR. It was a 3 credit hour course, which meant approximately 45 hours in class and whatever silly homework and projects we would have to do outside of class. I showed her the course description then showed my certifications for EMT-Basic, EMT-Paramedic, ACLS, PALS, CPR and my credentials as a certified first aid/CPR instructor. I literally taught this course in the military, *it would be silly if I had to take it, right?*

"Not the same thing" she told me.

Swallowing this rage was getting more difficult but I tried sticking to the logic route. With a voice that was almost quivering with anger I inquired, "I see that you accepted a biology class from a community college that I was at? So you don't have an issue transferring credits as long as they aren't from the military? You can clearly see that the course description for these courses are pretty much identical right?"

She responds simply with a very lazy, "yep."

"Okay, so what you are telling me is if I take a class wearing blue jeans it's good, if I take the EXACT SAME class wearing camouflage it's not good? That's what you're saying right now?"

"Pretty much, yeah." She responded without a single syllable of understanding or compassion. Just to clarify, I did a quick summary of our conversation with her.

"So you understand that I have successfully passed these classes, I have documentation of doing so. You, the transcript officer, can clearly see that I should receive credit for these courses but won't do so? I am going to be forced to retake these classes?"

"Yep"

"So what you are really saying is that this school knows that it has guaranteed tuition provided by the GI bill and wants to milk that? This is really pretty much about making more money for the school then?"

I couldn't believe it when she said yes. She flat out said yes.

My jaw hit the floor. I didn't know if I should be outraged or depressed or laugh at how incredibly ridiculous this entire thing was. I couldn't even get an elective credit for a basic fitness training class. I remembered a very good friend and fellow Ranger medic, Dave, telling me about how he had an issue with his transcripts right after getting out of the Army. He told me about how he became so upset that he literally knocked everything off the women's desk. This thought flashed through my mind in this moment. I realized that it wouldn't accomplish anything. This ignorant woman wasn't the problem. The problem is returning to a society that values turning a profit over supporting its guardians. I wasn't looking for a handout. All I wanted was to be given credit for work that I had already accomplished.

During my time as a student in Indiana, I would frequently have a professor say something absolutely backwards regarding the situation in Iraq and Afghanistan. I would attempt to repudiate it with firsthand experience but they always shot that down as unreliable. So I would go home and stay up all night researching every fact regarding the events they described in class from well-educated men who had written books but never been within a thousand miles of either theater. The next class I would drop more quotes from more well respected doctors that the teacher almost couldn't finish their lecture. They didn't respect my knowledge because I didn't have a degree. My experiences were not as credible to them as the quotes of old dead men. That is what they valued because that is what they knew; it was how they had lived their lives. As much as I wanted to give that woman a lesson in violence of action and on how to respect a person who has killed other people in an effort to secure her ability to sit in her fancy spinning chair, I opted to go the other route. I did my research and applied it.

I started crunching the numbers. There were a total of 22 credit hours that were transferable from my military service. The GI bill would cover the cost of these classes, at a cost of over $23,000 to the U.S. taxpayer. There is also a living stipend around $1,500 a month while you are in school full time. Let me say that again, your tax dollars are going to pay for classes that you already paid for with your tax dollars the first time that I took them. I am one veteran out of over a million using these benefits. If you are doing the math, that is over 20 billion dollars!

MSU Denver is also one of the least expensive schools that I have ever attended. If you apply the same numbers to a larger University, the numbers increase exponentially. I don't think it takes a fancy economics degree or seat in Congress to understand how absolutely absurd that is. Beyond the grotesque and egregious misuse of resources, it is a massive waste of time on the part of everyone involved. The veteran is now even more disgruntled that they are forced into a remedial course which has a tendency to create disruption in the class. Furthermore, veterans are allotted a total of 36 months of education benefits. If it takes more than the standard four years to complete your degree, you will be paying out of pocket.

At the time that my veteran education benefits expired, I was 15 credit hours shy of completing my degree and had retaken five classes that I had already successfully passed, albeit in camouflage, so they weren't "real." I sat through first aid and CPR every Wednesday night when I would typically be getting paid to coach classes. The class was taught by a woman with a master's degree in music, but who knew absolutely nothing about first aid. She had never been in an ambulance, never treated a patient, and had no clue how to answer the simplest of questions.

When asked by one of the students, "What is a contusion?"

She responded, "It's like when a bone is sticking out or something like that."

As I saw the young students pick up their pens to take a note I shouted, "Don't write that down! That couldn't be further from the truth."

Every week I attempted to help this poor woman who clearly had no idea what she was teaching. When I brought the issue up with one of the heads of the department, stating that I should not have to sit through this she said, "Well, you can help the teacher since she is less experienced."

So not only do I have to pay to sit through a course that I used to teach and pay for it, I get to do her job for her since she is incompetent. All the while losing money that I would be making coaching classes.

I wish that I could say that I toughed that one out. I wish I could say that I sat through every one of those terribly incorrect lectures and checked the box like a good little boy. I couldn't do it. The lesson that war taught me was simple yet impactful, war taught me that every moment is precious. It taught me that we might never get another day; we may not get another breath. I couldn't, in good conscience, sit through something that was supposed to be making me better, making me smarter, and knowing full well that it wasn't. More than one good man that I consider a brother no longer had the choice of how to live their life; they gave that up for this nation and those in it. I vowed to those men that I would never waste a day of my life, a life that had been spared.

This isn't education; it's a big game where I give my time so that this institution could turn a profit. Call me ideological but I had enough. That was one box I wasn't going to arbitrarily check. The military is in no way perfect but they do get a few things right. They put highly experienced instructors in front of disciplined students, teaching them things that they will absolutely need. If you have successfully shown proficiency in a course, you don't repeat it. I had my EMT going into the Army, because of this I was fast tracked through half of the combat medic course at Ft. Sam Houston. The Army didn't profit from me taking a class that I had already passed. Metropolitan State University of Denver does, however. For that reason, they will continue to disregard the knowledge, experience and sacrifice of men and women in uniform.

While I was repeating class after class at MSU, I was making legitimate progress in my professional life. We had opened the second gym location and had continued to increase membership. I was coaching as much as possible and began helping with programming and social media responsibilities. The two owners had mentioned to me that they wanted to bring me on as a partner. This would have been great news but I was still not in a place where I wanted that responsibility. I was still very tired from the battle that ensued over my previous gym and I didn't want to be back in that situation again.

Around the same time, I found out that one of my grandparents was having health issues. My father told me that it would be a good idea to get to New York to visit as soon as I could. I had to check in with my parole officer but didn't see it being an issue. I had to fill out a form requesting permission to travel from the assistant District Attorney in Jefferson County. A couple of days later, I got a call from my attorney stating that my ex wouldn't sign off on me leaving the state. This confused me greatly. She knew my grandparents. She had stayed at their farmhouse when we were still together. She knew the situation with the health issues and said that I shouldn't be allowed to go anywhere and that I should still be in jail. For the life of me, I couldn't put her reasoning into any logical format. She didn't want me around but didn't want me to leave.

After a conversation with my attorney, the Assistant District Attorney decided that my ex was being incredibly spiteful and unreasonable. She approved my request and in the process I learned something that would eventually help my case. I continued to show up to court appointments for several weeks after I returned from New York. I had taken a rather substantial loan from my father to cover the attorney fees but felt that the representation was worth it if I could avoid any further jail time. We hired a private investigator that was very helpful.

The private investigator introduced herself to my ex and asked a few questions that she recorded. The story that she told was different from the one that she had given on the police reports making her appear incredulous. During the court date that would determine if this would go to trial, the female prosecutor told my attorney that she was dropping the case. She said that it was absolutely ridiculous that I had been arrested in the first place and there was no way she would go to trial with my ex being her only witness after interviewing her a few times.

That was it. Just like that. After the time I spent in jail, having to check in multiple times per week and going through this whole process, it was over. The only thing left was the bill. In the end, I would have to make payments each month on the $15,000 tab I got from my attorney.

You would think that would have been the end of it. You would think that my ex would have felt that she had one and leave me to move on. She didn't. She needed to convince the world that she was a victim so she went to different CrossFit gyms and bad mouthed me. She told anyone that would listen that she had a restraining order against me, a fact that was completely untrue. She told people in the community where I worked that I was dangerous and abusive, exacerbating the negative stigma affixed to veterans.

It got to the point where I had gym owners, that I had never met, tell me that I wasn't welcome in their gyms. She still had my dog. She had won but it wasn't enough. She continued to assault my character from afar. Like mortar rounds raining down from a location out of sight, she tried to disrupt my life and there was nothing I could do. "Take the high road," my father always says. It went beyond turning the other cheek. The system had already shown me that it was going to take her side over mine. The fact that I was a combat veteran was enough to tilt the perception of the people she spoke with, making me guilty in their eyes.

There is a social heuristic that works against, not for those returning from war. There is an erroneous belief that because a person has done violence on behalf of a society, that they will turn that same violence on said society. Logically it makes no sense. These men have done things that they did not want to do in order to preserve the sanctity and peace of the people in their homeland. Why then, would they do harm to those who they were sworn to protect? It's not that soldiers want to kill others; the fact is their wish is to preserve the way of life to which they have become accustomed. Soldiers fight in faraway lands so that oppression never finds its filthy feet on the doorstep of their loved ones. Logic dictates that, when unprovoked, the combat veteran is the least dangerous individual on U.S. soil. Images in the media of a crazed veteran killing dozens of innocent people may fill seats in a theater but is so far from any logical truth that it is nefarious at best.

Chapter 18: Rooms of the House

Life has an interesting way of repeating itself. By early 2012, I was once again a gym owner and once again dating the woman with whom I was a partner. Things seemed to be going well, at first. She was an absolutely brilliant person with the unique ability to make me feel just as intelligent. Her jet-black curly hair was in stark contrast to her milky white skin and she had the eyes of a child. They were filled with a perfect blend of knowledge and curiosity. She seemed to challenge the way that I thought about things in a manner that no one else ever had. She was the inspiration that caused me to begin writing yet there was a very clear disconnect between our two personalities. She had a very timid demeanor and was completely opposed to conflict. Being engaged in an argument made her physically ill.

For the longest time, I thought that saying exactly what was on your mind meant that you are a good communicator. That, however, is not accurate. The way that you say those things plays as much of a part as the words themselves. I spoke aggressively because that is the way that I learned how to interact with those around me. It must be incredibly difficult for a woman that has never been around those conversations to understand when you bring a perceived tumultuous lexicon into the fold.

It was something that she could never quite get over. What a conversation was to me, was an argument to her. After dating for the better part of a year and living together for about a month, she up and left one day. She never told me where she was going or that she would be leaving. She just took her stuff and left while I was in class one day. She was the second person that I loved that could not understand who I was or how hard I was trying to be something different for her. She was the second person that I loved who walked out before I could figure it out, while I was screaming to be a part of a world that didn't understand my language.

When I fight, I fight with every bit of violence I can summon. When I run, I run until my legs give out and when I love, I love until it taxes the seams of my heart. Nothing is done half way, not even heartache. True or not, in my mind it seemed that there was no hope that there could ever be a woman that could possibly understand who I am and what I need. It seemed to me that many have tried, a few have come close but I am a difficult person to be with. I have the highest of expectations of those who would walk by my side. The brothers that I knew in the military were held to a certain standard. Regardless of personal hardship, adversity, or personal shortcomings, those individuals would be there for me. It's possible that this is an unreasonable expectation to have in a person that knows nothing of that lifestyle yet somehow those are the standards from which I cannot waiver.

The falling out between us meant that I would no longer be a partner in the gym that we owned together. I was bought out and once again, left looking for a path to follow. As fate would have it, an opportunity to open a new gym came quickly. I was able to partner with a few good friends and had a new place open in less than a month. I don't regret the decision to do so, however, the process was rushed, causing more unnecessary stress. Sitting idly by, however, was not an option. I am a man of action. When I see an opportunity, I go for it. Some may find that approach foolish, but it is a habit set forth from time spent in combat. He who waits, dies. Life seldom pauses at the convenience of the individual.

In the time between being forced out of one gym and opening another, I had a lot of downtime. I was between semesters in school and was asked by my roommate if I could write a story about my time as a medic for the popular website SOFREP. I gladly obliged and wrote my first short story, *Memoirs of an Army Ranger Medic*. It was published in three parts. Hundreds of positive comments came in about how good it was and that I should write more. While it did well to boost my morale during a trying time in my life, it also kicked up several memories that I had done well for years to suppress. The dreams that I hadn't had in years began to return and more of my nights were spent sitting alone with a glass of Jameson than sleeping.

Why did it still hurt so damn much? If time is supposed to heal all wounds, why wouldn't these ones approximate? Time doesn't heal wounds, whether they are physical or psychological. Being proactive and addressing those wounds, debriding them if necessary, is the only way to improve the chances they heal properly. I hadn't done that though. Over the past seven years, I had ignored those wounds and now they were infected and festering.

I had considered myself one of the lucky ones. I still had all my fingers and toes. I still had my eyesight and most of my hearing. Why, after all these years, were these things still haunting me? After all, every one of my friends seemed to have adjusted well. Most had been married and started families of their own by this point. Every time we would get together, they seemed happy and these were men that went through all I did and more. Was I so mentally weak that I was the only one after all these years that couldn't pin these demons to the ground?

Although it drudged up more painful memories than I cared for, writing became cathartic. It also gave me an excuse to reach out to friends that I hadn't spoken with in years. I was making every effort to be as accurate as possible and needed to confirm details with other guys that were there. It was easy to hear in their voice that simply having someone to recant the stories with was a huge help for them as well. It inadvertently became a series of therapy sessions for not just me, but my brothers on the other end.

Once again, life got crazy with owning a business and I wasn't able to write anything new for months. It seemed to really be the one thing that was starting to help and because of my other obligations I just didn't have the time or energy for it. These were the first steps that I seemed to be making in the right direction. The chaos of life, however, set up a blocking position.

An event called "Ranger Rendezvous," was quickly approaching and I couldn't wait. Every couple of years, all Rangers from every generation descend upon Fort Benning, Georgia for a massive reunion. In seven years, I never had the ability to make it to one but this year would be different. I told myself, no matter what I would be there. I was finally beginning to learn that being around those men was what I needed.

In true Ranger fashion, we drank more beer than we should have and told stories loud enough that the rest of the bar couldn't help but hear. A dozen tattooed, bearded, steely-eyed guys yelling and cursing at the bar tend to get a pass from the bouncer. So much so that when one very large, corn fed 23 year old that was currently serving as a sniper at 3rd battalion jokingly postured at me, I simply handed my drink to the door man and told the kid we were going outside. Every one of my friends tried to talk him out of it. They tried convincing him it was a really bad idea. I didn't expect him to back down. He was a Ranger after all. It's different when a college guy postures at you. Usually they don't actually want to fight. It's more of a peacock flashing his feathers. Rangers though, Rangers are a different breed. A Ranger will fight another Ranger, not because he is trying to prove something, but simply because he is bored.

A shame his ability didn't match his confidence. After about 30 seconds, a group of guys were trying to revive him and I was covered in his blood. My friend Matt, who was finishing medical school, stepped in, called me an idiot and finally got him to come to.

"Yeah... You're gonna need stitches." Matt slurred to the dazed young Sergeant. Not only did the bouncer not intervene he handed me my beer and we were allowed back in for last call. The next four days went by too fast and when I returned to Colorado, I had a newfound motivation to finish my book. I couldn't tell all of the stories of those men, but I could do my best. I took to finishing *Lest We Forget*, writing over 100 pages the following week. Rendezvous primed my writing but also opened my eyes to something that I lost sight of. I needed those guys in my life and whether or not they readily admitted it, they needed me too.

In addition to being an incredible motivator for my writing, the trip served to remind me of a promise that I made years before. When my friend James Regan was killed in Iraq, I vowed to live every day of my life to the fullest. I vowed that I would never waste what I had been given. Life is a precious gift, a gift that is taken from too many men that are better men than I can ever hope to be. Being unhappy and trying to carry on just making it to the next day is a slap in the face. I wasn't happy. Hell, I was miserable.

Something had to change. Enough time had passed allowing me to see a pattern. I would be doomed to keep repeating my mistakes if I didn't find their root.

The seventh anniversary of my separation from the military was quickly approaching and it was apparent that each passing year gave little amelioration from the scars of war. I denied their existence. All signs now pointed to mental sepsis. The wound had been allowed to fester and now its treatment would fall out of my scope of practice. I needed help. In August of 2013, nearly a decade after my final combat deployment, I finally decided to step up and admit to myself that I had post-traumatic stress. I had been denying the fact for so long that the simple act of self-admittance was a relief in and of itself.

The negative stigma affixed to such a designation had kept me from admitting its hold on me. I couldn't stand the thought of being labeled as having a disorder. No part of me felt sick or broken. Connotations of a crazed, disheveled vet, stammering to himself while begging for change danced in my head when such a term was used. That wasn't me. That isn't 99% of the people that have traumatic stress related issues.

I really wasn't sure what the process was for receiving help with matters like these. I looked at the model of receiving assistance for physical injuries from the VA and assumed that this was similar so I figured that the first step was to file a claim. Once the claim had been approved, then the veteran would be eligible for assistance. I enlisted the help of an agency called the Disabled American Veterans (DAV) to help with filing and processing the claim. There was no appointment necessary, just show up and get help with the paper work.

After a few hours in the waiting room, a gentleman my age called my name and took me back to his office. I told him what was going on and he made the process sound very simple. I was told that at this stage, I wouldn't need any documents and that the process would take about three months. At the time, three months seemed like a long time to wait considering the nature of the problem, but I had been dealing with it for so long that three more months wouldn't kill me. The appointment lasted for maybe three or four minutes. At no time was I asked for any supporting evidence or examples of reasons for the claim. I went home and began watching the mailbox.

After four and a half months, without receiving any notification, things were getting much worse. The holidays were never a good time and for some reason, this year seemed to be even more difficult. Trailers for the movie 'Lone Survivor' were being shown on a regular basis, bringing back details that I had done well to bury over the years. I wanted to remain proactive so I contacted the Veterans Affairs regional office. I explained how the DAV had helped me with the claim and informed me that it would take about three months before I would hear anything.

The woman on the other line kind of laughed and said that it was closer to a year for these sorts of things. I couldn't believe it. A year? The past four months had been hell waiting to talk with someone about what has been going on. When I explained that I couldn't wait another seven to eight months to talk with someone, she said that there was a chance that I wouldn't actually be talking to a doctor during the process of the claim. This struck me as incredibly odd. I asked how they could make the decision without a doctor's evaluation. She told me that they would be using the supporting evidence in the form that I submitted in order to determine my claim. This was in direct opposition to what the employee at the DAV had told me. There wasn't anything with that claim because I was told that I didn't have to submit anything.

My mind was spinning in every direction. I truly didn't know if I should laugh at the incompetence or scream from the rage I was feeling, or cry because of how damn lost I felt. The VA employee on the other end of the line told me that I could simply go to the VA's website and upload any documents that I have supporting my claim. When I asked specifically if doing this would in any way affect the amount of time my claim would take to process, I was told no. Being skeptical I asked again, "Are you sure that this isn't going to put me back at the end of the line?"

I was told with strict confidence that it would not, in any way, impact the timing on the claim. Within three days, I had written and submitted multiple narratives of my experiences along with documents supporting each of the stories. The following day, I called to ensure that the office where I sent them had received the documents that I had faxed. I wasn't surprised by what I heard next. By this point I was accustomed to getting jarringly conflicting information from the same organization. No I wasn't surprised, that isn't to say that it didn't completely enrage me.

When I asked if the office had received the copies of my documents I was told that not only could they not confirm anything to me but that by submitting new documents I changed the status of my claim, sending it to the back of the line. I once again felt my right eye tick. I attempted to explain the situation in hopes that something could be done. I told her that not more than a week ago I was assured the opposite of what she was now confirming. There was a steady stream of statistics flowing from my end of the line to hers.

She quickly became aware that these types of things are the reasons why veterans were so upset. No one was actually helping us. Twenty-two veterans a day commit suicide. Largely in part because when they ask for help from the one organization whose sole purpose is to provide assistance to veterans they shit all over them. No one is on the same page about anything and the people that it impacts are guys like me. She responded with, "Sir, I'm only allowed to spend six minutes on the phone with each caller so if you don't have any further questions I am going to have to let you go."

That is real. That is what I was told. Seven years of treading water by myself in a mental ocean of anguish and solitude, I finally call out for help and I am told that I'm only authorized six fucking minutes of assistance. I didn't want a hand out. I didn't want sympathy. I didn't want pity. I just wanted to get this on record so that I could finally talk with someone. I just wanted to be able to live my life the way that I used to live it. Nothing more, nothing less. I just wanted to be like every other well-adjusted person that never breathed the stench of war and all the hell it brings.

I unloaded every bit of pain and anger and experience to that woman over the phone. It wasn't because I thought she could do anything about it, it was because it had been boiling in me for so long that the time had simply come for it to froth over. It wasn't some violent mass murder the way that those fear-mongers in the media will pedal that veterans are dangerous. It wasn't even in a threatening tone. Her six minutes just seemed to be an analogous trigger. It felt like the past seven years where the American people's attitude was that they tolerated your voice for a few minutes but were unable and unwilling to commit any more time or attention to the assimilation of the war fighter. Support your troops as long as it doesn't interfere with your cozy life. Shake their hand, smile, say good job, but make no attempt to assist them with anything. Ignore their applications for work. Tell them that you "don't want to hear about it" when they bring up something they saw in Iraq. Give them the designated six minutes of obligatory time and move on.

I believe vehemently that if our nation actually cared at all about its veterans, that there would be a program in place to effectively reintegrate them into society. The cases and severity of things like post-traumatic stress would be overwhelmingly reduced if we as a nation followed the lead of so many other countries' model. The majority of everything that I have dealt with and watched my friends deal with would never happen if there was an effective system in place immediately upon a soldiers return from combat.

Instead, seven years later, I found myself emotionally breaking down to a complete stranger over the phone.

Doing so led to two things. First, I felt slightly better having expressed how I felt to another human being who, by the end of the call, seemed genuinely sympathetic. The second, she informed me that my understanding of the process was not correct. She said that all I have to do is call and make an appointment with the mental health clinic at the VA medical center and tell them that I would like to talk to someone.

I felt a little foolish being told this now, after everything that I had already gone through but simultaneously felt a renewed sense of hope that I would be able to actually get help this week instead of waiting another year. I called the VA medical center immediately after getting off the phone. My newfound excitement was short lived as the gentleman on the other line told me that I, in fact, could not make an appointment over the phone. I would have to come into the office downtown and fill out a preliminary form then an appointment could be made. This sounded all too familiar. Fill out a form and wait for someone to get around to helping you.

It didn't matter. Now more than ever I knew that I needed help. It is possible that there isn't a single place on earth that I have a greater disdain for than the mental health clinic at the VA, but that is where help was supposed to be so that is where I was going. The next day I drove through the city, drove around for an hour looking for a parking spot and walked into purgatory. The waiting room of the mental health clinic was packed with veterans of all ages and branches of service. All of whom looked like whatever treatment they had been receiving wasn't working. There was this collective dull, melancholy look on their faces.

I requested the necessary form from the man behind the plate glass window. He looked up from his archaic computer just long enough to slide me a clipboard. "Here. Fill this out." He murmured.

The questions all had a consistent theme. Are you a drunk that's looking to hurt yourself or someone else? It felt more like a perpetuation of a negative stereotype than a screening. I refused to answer half of them. One, because I philosophically opposed the way these questions were presented and two, because I wasn't about to write on a document that I was thinking about hurting someone.

Apparently the way to fast track yourself into seeing a doctor is to refuse to answer the questions on that form. Apparently that must mean that you are an alcoholic that wants to kill yourself. Within two minutes, a woman approached me the way we used to advance on a rattlesnake we were trying to remove from someone's backyard when I was a firefighter. I'm sure the tone she used was intended to sound comforting and empathetic, but it came off as incredibly condescending. It was a testament to how much of a disconnect there is between the people working in these environments and the people that they are trying to help. I've fought two wars; don't talk to me like I'm a kindergartner who just peed his pants.

At this point, I was taken back to a tiny room, complete with flickering fluorescent lights and one piece of generic art on the white cinder-block wall. It resembles a well-kept jail cell with a desk in the corner.

I was told to take a seat with my back to the sidewall as two older ladies box me in and begin asking me a series of questions in the same tone of voice. It had been a long time since I had felt that uncomfortable. I explained what had been going on and what had brought me to this point. The women almost seemed surprised that I was able to clearly and poignantly articulate my experiences, going as far as to describe what I felt the root of each feeling was. It was as though they expected anyone going through these things to be completely brain dead. Multiple times they complimented me on my vocabulary and understanding of how my own mind works. Even now, people surrounded me that had absolutely no concept of what a special operations medic was and the amount of adversity that they were required to overcome just to achieve that title.

Both women agreed that I should see a specific doctor who had apparently worked with "guys like me" before. They also agreed that the sooner and greater frequency the better. I had already taken time away from work for this and would have to do the same later this week for my first actual appointment. I explained that wouldn't be too much of an issue because this was absolutely my first priority. Two days later I found myself circling the same neighborhood searching for a spot. I was terrified about what was about to happen. I had been running from these things for so long and now the time had come to confront them. I had no idea what was about to happen but I had to believe that it whatever transpired was what was best for me, that it was a step toward healing and in turn finally feeling at home. It was terrifying. The long walk from my truck to the front door was done on wobbling legs. The anxiety I felt on my first combat mission in Afghanistan paled in comparison to what I was embarking on now.

I arrived fifteen minutes early, checked in and waited. I was reading *Paradise Lost* and didn't realize that I had been there for nearly half an hour. My appointment was supposed to start fifteen minutes ago. I approached the man behind the glass and asked if anything was wrong. He didn't understand so I reiterated that my appointment was supposed to start at the top of the hour. "That's odd. Well the doctor should be out any minute now. Just hold tight."

I sat back down and continued my efforts to dissect Milton's brilliance. By half past, I inquired once again. Muffled by the glass, the man sees me standing in front of him again, "She still hasn't come to get you yet? Let me give her a call."

After a few more minutes a lady came out from a back office with a rushed look and asked if I'm Leo. By this point I was pretty annoyed. She told me that she didn't know that she had an appointment this hour. Even though it bothered me to no end to not only be left waiting, having the majority of my time wasted in the waiting room, what really got to me was that she called me "her appointment." I was led down a corridor to a slightly larger office than the last one I sat in with a slightly larger, less organized desk illuminated by the same flickering fluorescent lights. I'm sat down with my back to the door as some papers were shuffled around. While the woman begins organizing her desk with her back to me she asks what is going on.

This caught me off guard a little. She wasn't even looking at me when she asked the first question. It was almost as though I was intentionally being made to feel as uncomfortable as possible. I couldn't tell if this was some kind of tactic or the level of treatment at the VA was really that terrible. It wouldn't take long to realize that it was the latter of the two. By the end of the session, she had bragged to me that she knew all about the Rangers and how they work. She brandished a plaque that she had been given by some Ranger officer that I'd never heard of. Her feeble attempt at trying to establish credibility was another stone on the wall that I was building in resistance to this approach. As I left the parking lot, I felt a degree of anger that was rare for me. I'm not sure if something I said opened me up a little, or if I was just completely pissed about how the session went, but I wanted someone to give me a reason to open their skull as I drove home. I wanted someone to cut me off so I would have a reason to pull them from their car and make a stain on the road with them.

I had to go directly from that appointment to coach a group of athletes at my gym. When one of them asked me a question, and then talked over me as I answered them, I lost my cool. I stopped everything and very aggressively made the point that if you are going to ask me to do something, or explain something, at least have the courtesy to shut up when I am speaking. It was the Sergeant Jenkins that had been suppressed for years coming out. I no longer cared about hurting someone's feelings, I was passed that point. I had just barely been afloat for years and somehow now, with the compounding of all that had occurred, I finally started to drop below the surface.

Despite the fact that it seemed like a complete waste of time, I returned a couple of days later for another appointment. This time she was only five minutes late, a drastic improvement. Once again, I was sat down with my back to the door, an action that increased my anxiety further. She began telling me about a new revolutionary way to treat Post-Traumatic Stress. The woman pulled out a small device with two wires attached. At the end of the wires were small, egg-like objects that I was instructed to place in the palm of each hand. After turning the machine on, she told me to think back to the most traumatic event during my time in the military. As I tried to think of one single incident she turned on the machine. The objects began to rhythmically vibrate in my palms. She sat there staring at me attentively to see if my demeanor changed. After a few minutes she asked if I was feeling any better.

"No!" I replied. "What the fuck is this nonsense?"

She told me that it defragged the memories so that I could process them. All I could think of was what a load of shit this all was. She didn't know anything about my memories and she thought a vibrating rock was going to solve my problems. What I need is for people to care as much about the war as they do about reality television, what I need is to get a good night's sleep, what I need is to never come back to this place ever again!

Chapter 19: Nobody, Not Even the Rain

The movie *Lone Survivor* had just come out and even though I told myself I wasn't going to watch it, I felt that I had an obligation to. The hype was mounting and it was being touted as one of the most accurate military movies out there. My first book had recently been published and already thousands of people had read about my platoon's involvement with the search and rescue mission that we conducted for the four Navy SEALs compromised on Operation Red Wings. Sadly, that search and rescue turned into a recovery operation. Countless people asked me about the movie before it was even released. I wasn't the only one searching the mountains for those guys, far from it. There were multiple units doing a lot of hard walking. I just seemed to be the only one talking about it. A friend sent me a link to a site where I could watch the entire movie at home. That night I sat down with a tall glass of Jameson and commenced opening up a scar that never quite healed right.

From the opening scene to the conclusion, the film was riddled with inaccuracies. The objections that I held weren't based on conjecture from my experience. The largest glaring deceptive exaggerations were in direct contradiction to historical fact. The mission's after action review had been significantly modified when the book was written and now the version of the story told in the book was manipulated even further in the film.

I received countless emails from friends that I was on the mission with asking what was going on with the accuracy of the film. I felt indirectly exploited by the whole thing. Those making the movie, in all of their infinite wisdom, decided to bastardize something that didn't need to be inflated. The core of that story stands on its own. Four men gave everything for one another. Four brothers defending each other with every ounce of their souls. Beyond that, sixteen more men perished in an effort to come to their aid. Additionally, over a hundred other men risked everything for the sake of their return, dead or alive. That is a truly special thing and deserves its day on the big screen.

What disturbed me the most was that everyone was talking about how the movie was so accurate. The entire world would now believe that it was the truth when the film was more Hollywood than reality. The Taliban body count was grossly exaggerated in an effort to sell more seats in theaters and an entire battle scene that never took place was added for effect. One

Hollywood director was able to change history. He was able to create enough of a spectacle and sell it as the truth so that an entire generation's concept of an event would be forever manipulated. It was a damn propaganda tool.

Think about how incredibly disturbing that is for a moment. Someone with enough influence contorts the nature of an event enough and sells it to an impressionable audience as the truth. That audience is now radicalized in the cause against an enemy. Does that sound familiar at all? This is the same tactic used by radical Imams in Madrasas to indoctrinate and manipulate children and young adults into being suicide bombers.

Once again, I witnessed a large part of the country see this movie, take it as the truth and utter absolutely ignorant statements like, "we should bomb every last one of those fuckers." *Really?* By "we" you mean another wave of 18 and 19-year-old American soldiers should be sent to kill other 18 and 19 year olds because you watched a movie that was highly inflated, just so they can return to a country where the government that sent them to war won't support them when they return?

That is a great plan, one perpetuated by those in the media that care more about ratings or ticket sales than telling the real story of war. War isn't a fucking movie. It costs a lot more than a few trillion dollars. It costs more than buildings and bombs. It costs more than the discomforts that soldiers feel when they are away from their families. War is the single most disgusting, vile plague in human history. It is the greatest argument against ours being an advanced civilization and will never end as long as there are opportunistic pieces of shit in our government and media willing to sell it for their own personal gain. To those people, I say, *Fuck You... you are the real terrorist and we the people are sick of your shit!*

I wrote an article called, *Lone Survivor and the Truth* for a website called, *The Havok Journal*. In it, I laid out why I was upset about the movie. It was published and within a matter of hours had thousands of shares on social media sites. Within a few days, over 100,000 people had read the piece and many of them were commenting. I was called a coward and told that I had no moral compass. I was called a piece of shit and referred to as a REMF (Rear Echlon Motherfucker). While more people had something good to say than bad, it was still crazy that I was coming under attack from anyone. People who had never been to war had the audacity to publicly ridicule me for my sentiment on a mission that I was a part of.

I spent years running from these problems. I ignored them or tried to passively drown them in whiskey. Enough was enough; I decided to engage them head on. I decided to begin writing about every one of the most painful things that I had for so long been burying. It was time to bite the bullet and finally debride the wound. I set out in an endeavor that I knew would be terribly painful. Now beyond the pain of having to relive those moments there were people in this country, people who have never served a day in their lives, calling me a piece of shit for doing so. That isn't an isolated incident. That is a direct result of a society that completely undervalues its warrior class.

How can a man that seeks warmth under the blanket of protection and freedom that is provided by another man call his integrity into question? Because we allow him to. It's sad but true, yet it hasn't always been that way. Should veterans get a free pass? Absolutely not, but what they should get is credit for their experience.

I responded to each of those individuals personally through private messages providing my home address and invited them to express their disapproval to me personally. Of course, they never accepted the offer because they are cowards. Coward is a harsh word so we mask it with others in our lexicon to soften the blow. We no longer allow children to engage in full contact sports in fear that they may become hurt. We give trophies to every kid on the team because heaven forbid they think that they are inferior to someone else. We stroke a false sense of steam to generations of individuals who grow up to pick fights over the Internet but don't have the stomach for actual conflict.

While I do not believe that we are a nation of cowards I do believe that the weak willed vituperations of those who have been made and kept free by the exertions of better men than themselves have become the guidelines that we must follow. We, the veterans of war, are such a numerical minority that we can never be considered right in how we view society. Since the overwhelming majority of our nation consists of people without the sense of duty, purpose or courage to fight for what is just, we are doomed to conform to their concept of social and worldly correctness. In this, the portion of society that has risked the most will forever have the least influence in the principles that guide it.

We seem doomed to assimilate into a weaker, less-organized culture that is lacking the altruism and sacrifice that was once the bedrock of our existence. In an effort to achieve gainful employment, be successful in relationships and not be looked at with disdain, we must abandon the very qualities that have kept us alive. Somehow we have to find an appropriate balance. Well, I've never been very good at balance. I've always been more of an all or nothing kind of guy.

Chapter 20: The Last Lost Continent

Trudging through two feet of snow, I reached for the frozen handle of my Dodge Dakota, hours before the sun would make its presence felt. Knocking the obnoxious, freezing white substance from my shoes a single thought changed my trajectory irrevocably.

"I don't want to go to work today."

That was it. I don't know a single adult that hasn't had the exact same thought echo through their own subconscious. As the frozen air blasting through the vents converted to a temperature capable of melting the frost on the windshield, I was reminded of a simple promise that I had made to a friend years before. I wasn't there when James was killed in Iraq but I remember the moment that I heard the news. I remember the absolute abyss that I fell into in the days and weeks afterward. In the wake of that tragedy I made a promise to my friend and every one of my brothers that didn't come home from war that I would do everything in my power to honor their memories. I would do that by living life to the fullest. Too many of the best and brightest of our time were robbed the opportunity to choose how they spend their twenties and beyond. The best way that I could honor them would be to never waste a day being miserable if I could avoid it.

As my headlights illuminated the path to my business, the solution was clear. Life is too short, too damn precious to spend so much as one day of it miserable. Before arriving at my destination, less than three minutes later, the plan had already developed. The next few months would be as transformative as any I have ever had. Something in me was screaming for movement, a cry that I could not ignore.

It was a huge gamble when I left the fire department to join the military at twenty years old and it seemed to pay off. Because of that decision, I was able to see parts of the world that few will ever experience. I met men that became my brothers, men that no matter what I could rely on when things got tough. Now I was faced with another crossroad.

Writing had become a new outlet; my most effective way of confronting the wounds of war. It was highly cathartic to be the creator of conversations on issues impacting today's combat veterans. Expressing thoughts and emotions through words seemed to not only be a healthier way of coming to terms with certain traumatic events than my previous avenues; I also seemed to have a talent for it. I was unsure at the time if I could make a living writing but I did know that writing appeared to be a way for me to reclaim the life I once knew.

It was clear that I wasn't going to be taken seriously as a writer if I continued to cling to my old identity. The change needed to be as drastic and complete as the flames of the Phoenix, emerging in vibrant color from the dismal ashes of its past. I chose to purge everything that wouldn't fit into a single backpack and set forth to a place where I was once as happy as I have ever been.

The plan was fairly simple: sell everything. What I couldn't sell I would give away. I bought a one-way ticket to a country where I didn't know the language, where I didn't know a single other person. I had visited Costa Rica about five years before with my ex-fiancé. It seemed so peaceful there. The people were kind and the national motto, "Pura Vida" seemed to echo the lifestyle that I desired.

I needed a place where I could silence my own mind. I needed a place where I could do nothing but sit and think about all of the good and bad that has come from my time in the military and all of the decisions that I have made since. Why was every relationship a failure? Why couldn't I hold a job? Why did I look at so many people with such hate for no real reason? Could I still focus my mind and survive as a writer? I needed to answer these questions. The VA wasn't going to help me, that was clear now. By in large, society had no interest in my struggles. It was on me to change my direction. I had to take responsibility for my own healing. South was the direction of choice.

February 24th marked the beginning of an incredible journey. I broke ties with the life that I had spent years building in hopes that I could preserve my own life. A new set of challenges arose as I navigated my way through a new and strange place. I was seeking comfort in the unknown and unknowable. Leaving the dark Denver winter in pursuit of a never ending supply of Vitamin D seemed to electrify my outlook on all the wonderful possibilities that life wishes to bestow upon us.

By April 24th, my feet were dangling from a beachside hammock as the taste of fresh mango danced on my tongue. The sun had only just peaked over the lush green treetops an hour before but I had already managed to catch a spectacular solo surf session. For the first hour of the day, the ocean belonged to me. The warm ocean breeze dried the salt water from my skin as I sifted through the messages on my iPad. A picture message from my former roommate and fellow Ranger, Iassen, snapped me back to reality. It was a letter from the VA stating that my claim for PTSD was denied.

None of the documentation that I sent in was ever taken into consideration and I was never given the opportunity to see a mental health specialist for a review of my current issues, which is protocol. Another letter had also been sent around the same time stating that I had ten days to respond and schedule my appointment for evaluation. The postmark on the letter was seven days after the deadline to respond. I couldn't believe it. Even if I had been in the States, that letter would have somehow had to have been delivered a week before it was sent for me to be able to respond in time.

As soon as I could get to a phone I called to find out what was going on. The woman on the other line told me that despite it being past the deadline to reply I could still schedule an appointment. She told me that due to her backlog she hadn't gotten around to closing my claim. For once, the painfully slow manner in which the VA handles their business played to my advantage. I knew I was going to have to fly back to Denver for the appointment and asked what day and time was available. I was told that I couldn't be given a specific day right now but it would be for the first week of June.

I agreed to be in Denver for the entire week. A few days prior to the appointment, I called back and confirmed the day and time. I flew back to Denver and despite being sent to the wrong hospital I finally was able to see a doctor. After less than five minutes, he began a sales pitch about how helpful psychotropic drugs can be.

Fuck this guy! was all I could think. This doctor had taken no subject or objective notes, made no assessment and jumped directly to the "plan" portion of the SOAP note. There is a direct correlation between the increases of psychiatric medication in the military and the suicide rate, and now this doctor was trying to force feed them to me without taking my background. Repeatedly, I denied his suggestion for the chemicals he was pushing and repeatedly he suggested them. He insisted that he knew what I was going through, a notion I found quite absurd considering we had just met. I was made to go through a series of what can only be described as remedial brain tests.

The way it works is you have to have to be near brain dead in order for the VA to admit that you have any service connected disability claim for mental health issues. The truth is I know plenty of guys that grind through their day-to-day lives, who hide their severe traumatic stress. The human mind is an amazing, ever evolving, mystery. The way a raging river will find a way around obstructions so will the human brain. The implication that you have to be retarded to suffer from severe PTSD is not just asinine, it is insulting.

According to the VA website, for a 50% rating the veteran must meet the following criteria:

"Occupational and social impairment with reduced reliability and productivity due to such symptoms as: flattened affect; circumstantial, circumlocutory, or stereotyped speech; panic attacks more than once a week; difficulty in understanding complex commands; impairment of short- and long-term memory (e.g., retention of only highly learned material, forgetting to complete tasks); impaired judgment; impaired abstract thinking; disturbances of motivation and mood; difficulty in establishing and maintaining effective work and social relationships"

Because of the way that the VA assesses combat veterans with post-traumatic stress, it has become common for people to exaggerate the state of their condition. I've heard of organizations coaching veterans to intentionally arrive for their compensation and pension appointment unkempt in order to suggest an inability to fit in with society. People play up their symptoms in order to obtain a higher disability percentage and in turn a larger monthly payout. In doing so, the curve that other veterans are graded on becomes altered making it even more difficult for them to receive the help that they so desperately need.

Some of my best friends in the world are walking around suffering more and more with each passing day because they refuse to walk into that office and play the game. They refuse to act crazy for the doctor in order to get the attention that they need. After years living with civilians some of these men haven't assimilated one bit and they are suffering from a level of emotional pain that few can comprehend. Their survival has been dependent on adaptation. In public, they adopt the vibrant colors of a chameleon in an effort to blend in with the society that doesn't understand them. Once at home, the true dark colors return. All the pain, anguish, desperation, fear, and addiction is suppressed so as to not upset the 99.5% of citizens that refused to serve. We become experts at hiding that so we can survive. For most of us, that is all we are doing, surviving.

When asked, I answered honestly as to the events of the past decade. When asked what single event was the most traumatic, I said truthfully that it would be impossible it pick one. I highlighted a few missions that seemed to stand out as well as the current situations that trigger them. I discussed the inability to maintain my relationships as well as the troubles with finding and maintaining employment. At the end of the hour, the doctor tried one more time to push the psychotropic drugs on me, to which I declined. His last statement was, "When you get the money, try not to spend it on alcohol."

That was the government's solution for treatment, drugs that will increase the probability that I kill myself or a monthly check. I'm not sure how either of those things equates to healing. Neither helps the root of the problem. Perhaps that's the point, maintain the problem and continue to profit from it.

Two months after that appointment, I once picked up the phone in an effort to be proactive. When I asked about the status of my claim the voice on the other end of the line stated simply and calmly, "Your claim was denied on April 24th, can I help you with anything else?"

I had to laugh. I wasn't surprised, not anymore. I explained the timeline of everything that had transpired with my claim over the course of the previous eleven months. Through the course of the conversation, I found out that the voice on the other end of the line was a Marine. His was the first concerned tone I had heard so far. I could hear him relate to every bit of the struggle as though he had just experienced it himself. The young Marine told me that he could see the notes made by the doctor that I had seen back in June and that there was absolutely no doubt to the legitimacy of my claim. He instructed me that I needed to fill out a notice of disagreement form, VA Form 21-0958 in order for my claim to become active again. Less than 24 hours after that phone call I submitted the necessary documents and waited.

Five weeks later, I once again decided to be proactive and call the VA. Following the standard forty-minute hold time I finally had a person on the line. When I asked about the status of my claim the voice on the other end of the line stated simply and calmly, "Your claim was denied on April 24th, can I help you with anything else?"

I asked if they had received my notice of disagreement. "No I don't see that. Where did you send it to?"

"I sent it to the address provided by the last VA representative I talked to which was ......"

"Oh, I don't know why they would have told you that. It should have gone... You may have to resend that. Is there anything else I can help you with?"

I lost my cool. "No, what I would like for you to help me with is the claim that I submitted over a fucking year ago!"

"Well, if I could just wiggle my nose like Bewitched then I would, but last time I checked I'm not magic."

Her condescending tone elevated my anger to an odd state of calmness. She wasn't going to help me. Finding someone at the VA willing and capable of actually helping was as about as common as a five leaf clover. I was upset because she wasn't helping. That is when I realized that it wasn't up to her to help me. I had been walking on a tight rope for eight years. I was trying so desperately to clench the pride that I felt in what I had helped to accomplish while simultaneously trying to forget the parts that empowered my demons.

She wasn't going to be able to help me with that. I realized in that moment that I would never fully assimilate. I will never be understood, merely tolerated, by the majority of society. The way I had done countless times with physical cuts and lacerations, it was up to me to debride this wound. First, I had to understand it. I had to track the cavitation of the mental bullet hole. No more running from it. No more pretending that I'm strong enough to endure the weight of it in solitude.

As I sat listening to another La Dispute song I realized that I had already done that. I already exposed the wound. I already scrubbed it and redressed it. I've done everything in my power to ensure that it heals. I've traveled through over two dozen countries this year alone in pursuit of some form of enlightenment through solitude. I've partnered with a fellow Ranger in a business whose mission is empowering our fellow veterans by giving them a voice. I've helped raise tens of thousands of dollars for organizations like Gallantfew.org, who pair veterans with local mentors. I've showed the world my wounds and those who have shared them in silence have supported me every step of the way. I had been stumbling through life for so long, attempting to come to understand these demons that somehow along the way I came to terms with them.

I didn't realize it at the time, but doing things like organizing Ranger breakfasts and staying on the phone all night with a suicidal brother were actually helping me heal. Pills didn't do that, alcohol didn't do that, shutting myself off didn't do that, being there for my brothers did. Sure it has taken the better part of a decade to regain that crucial sense of purpose but I'm okay with that. I still exude the same high degree of esprit de corps as I did on the day that I donned my tan beret eleven years ago, but I have found a new mission worthy of applying my motivation. Each and every day I am able to connect with more people like me. I can see it in their eyes and hear it in their voices that they too long for the same things that I do.

When I was presented with the opportunity to travel through the US and beyond with a fellow Ranger veteran on a mission to raise money for struggling veterans, I immediately jumped on a plane. With the help of our veteran network we were able to raise well over twenty thousand dollars and travel nearly 8,000 miles with nothing more than a hundred dollars and a backpack. That experience taught me so many things, at the top of the list was the fact that when we support one another nothing is impossible.

Since concluding that trip I have continued to travel, making my first complete lap around the world earlier this year, visiting over two dozen countries. Some people have looked at this journey as form of self-treatment, but that isn't accurate. Traveling hasn't helped me heal anymore than running all of those miles did. No, I travel because I feel at ease doing so. I don't need a new place in the same way that I don't need a pill. I wander this amazing, chaotic spinning chunk of rock because life is too short not to. One day my bones will be too brittle to ascend the winding staircases of castles in foreign lands. I move because movement is life and I intend to live the shit out of it, all of it, until it has dried, crumbled and dissipated in the wind like a late autumn leaf. But that, that is a journey for another time on a different set of pages.

Chapter 21: Never Come Undone

Is this it? Is this the conclusion? Is this where I am supposed to wrap everything up with a pretty little bow? What is the best way to do that? Perhaps I could take this time to highlight the 22 veterans a day that are killing themselves. That would be over 7,200 since I started writing this book less than a year ago. That is twice the human life lost on 9/11 and more than we lost in Iraq or Afghanistan in over a decade of war. Since starting this project 11 months ago, two of those 7,200 were personal friends that I served with. They had wives and children.

We have a Veteran Affairs department that created a fake waiting lists that resulted in the deaths of dozens of veterans so a few opportunistic ass holes could score a cash bonus. Over 60,000 men and women who served this great nation will sleep exposed to the elements tonight because they are homeless. It is easier to receive government assistance as an undocumented immigrant than as a combat veteran. I'm not an educated man, I'm just another blue-collar veteran of two foreign wars; the son of a fireman. I'm not going to sit here and pretend like I have some golden ticket to making life easier as a veteran. I have, however, made a few observations after tripping over just about every stone in the road along my journey.

Sometimes I don't want to assimilate. Hell, most times I don't care to be a part of what is left of this country. That is sad, I know. But it is how I feel. Often times I wish that I had never had come home. Coming home meant expectations. It meant having to be subordinate to inferior men. It meant having to explain unexplainable things, wearing a smile on my face while I was screaming inside and being away from the only people that have ever seen me at my very best. Every day, I have been reminded that I will never mean as much to anyone as I meant to those men.

I did come home, though. In doing, so I brought with me a responsibility to carry the memories of those who didn't. When I volunteered for service, I unknowingly volunteered for a lifetime of responsibility. The same way that as a sergeant, I was tasked with passing my experience and knowledge to those who would follow in my footsteps, so too is it my responsibility to stand ready to pull up my fellow veterans.

Some veterans have deeper scars than others. There is some absurd belief held by many combat veterans that because they themselves are not experiencing difficulties, no one else should be either. As a result, we begin to cannibalize one another. I hear the sentiment echoed almost on a daily basis of "suck it up and drive on," from one veteran to another. There is a belief that discussing issues facing our community translates to some form of weakness. The bravest men I have ever known not only charged full speed into a wall of bullets in Iraq, they came home and said, "I'm having some issues right now and I need a little help."

That is true courage. Asking for help is one of the most difficult things for people like us but often times it is the only way that we can heal. It would be difficult to argue that the wounds of war exist solely in a physical dimension. I do not believe that having symptomatic stress associated with traumatic events is the same as having a disorder, but I understand having these memories embedded in an ill equipped person's mind can make life incredibly difficult. The way and place where those memories seer themselves into our memory is different than other accumulated memories. As a result our body's endocrine system (hormones) can be affected. Things like adrenal fatigue can mimic depression. Recent studies have shown Vitamin D can be helpful in offsetting those hormonal imbalances.

There is no assimilation without healing. There are countless ways that a veteran can coup with the turmoil of war. Some are healthier than others. Personally, I made the mistake of thinking that alcohol was an appropriate therapist. Attempting to sweat out your demons can be effective until you sustain an injury that keeps you from self-help. Throwing yourself into your work so that you are so busy in an effort to occupy your demons is also only effective for as long as you can keep a suicide pace. When you slow down, and you will slow down, all of the months and years of pain will crash on your shores like a tsunami.

The two primary ways that the VA is choosing to deal with veterans returning from war is either with talk therapy or psychotropic drugs. I can't speak for everyone, but of all of the combat veterans that I have ever spoken with about talk therapy, only one or two have ever been willing enough to try it. I don't want to talk with someone that has no clue what I've been through and I sure as hell don't want to sit in a group of strangers every Tuesday and Thursday at 6pm and listen to everyone talk about how hard their week was. Bottom line is that a Band-Aid only works if you are willing to apply it and no Band-Aid is going to stop a major hemorrhage. As far as pushing mind-altering drugs on veterans, there is money in pharmaceuticals. For that reason, they will keep trying to cram them down our throats despite having evidence that they do more harm than good.

It is important to have as many tools available as possible. The most effective one is your network. You may not realize it, but as a veteran, you have access to more resources than you could possibly imagine. I'm not talking about government programs. The people you served with sacrificed a great deal to protect you. They are invested in your health and success as a result. We have to be able to rely on one another. There are more chances every single day to elevate your fellow veterans than most people realize. Instead we tend to demean and insult. In doing so we succeed in inhibiting our own social elevation.

Retired Navy SEAL and personal friend, Mikal Vega, has created a website with programs designed with great ideas for helping with the healing process called, vitalwarrior.org. Likewise friend and fellow Ranger, Karl Monger, has a site dedicated to linking up new veterans with mentors in their areas called gallantfew.org. Personally, the most helpful tool throughout this process has been simply to be around other people like me; people that understand. Concepts like "Ethos before Ego" established by Boone Cutler emphasize the need for veteran organization unity.

For Mikal Vega, his healing has come through nontraditional and progressive methods like InfraRed Spectrum therapy, acupuncture, and Kundalini Yoga. Other friends have taken to writing some of the most amazing poetry I have ever had the pleasure of reading, while others find solace in farming.

Whatever tools you choose, it is important to have several and to keep your friends close. They will be your biggest allies. Some will have a perceivably easier transition than others. Some will have a career and family waiting for them. For those of us watching life go by through the tinted green glass of a Jameson bottle it is easy to assume they are without discomfort. For some reason we all compartmentalize our pain. We look to others and say, "They have their shit together and I'm a mess. I'm not going to interrupt all of the good in their lives with my problems. Then we bury it. It doesn't mean that it isn't difficult for them too. They often just hide that pain a little better.

In writing all of this, I have attempted to be a voice for my fellow veterans. I have bled into the keyboard in an effort that you could feel my pain. I have drowned my demons in copious amounts of whiskey numbing the pain that arose from remembering all of these moments. But I'm not the voice of every veteran. When I started writing, I wanted you to be able to hand this book to your loved ones and say, "This is what it feels like. I can't put it in words because it hurts too much but this is what it feels like." I can't be your words though. This was my experience returning from war. I know that yours may have been different. That's why you have to find your own voice. You have to find your own way to heal. Above all else, if you take one thing from these pages, please know this: you are not alone!

There are generations of war fighters that wake up and go through the motions every day because they can't seem to detach themselves from the day that they carried it all. We all live in some shade of that grey. You are not alone and neither am I. We have each other. It's because I have you that I am still alive to write this and I will never stop being thankful for that. The days may come when things seem insurmountable. When they do, I remember that because of you, I am batting 1.000 on those days. I have survived 100% of every day that I wanted to end my own life and if you are reading this, so have you. That is how strong you are. You have never failed in that regard.

My brothers, I am here for you because you were here for me. Whether you knew them or not, someone at one point died for you, now it's time for you to live for them. Find happiness in an otherwise dismal situation and know that you have all the light of the world in your capabilities. By simply picking up the phone and removing yourself from isolation you have the power to save a life, if not yours than possibly theirs. If you don't think you have an ear, you do. I've said it before and I will say it now, "Here I am, send me."

Here I am, call me, message me, and email me. I don't need to know you, you're my family. First we must heal, then we can think about assimilation.

At the time of this book going to print the VA has yet to acknowledge any potential detrimental effects of my service. The VA has made no attempt to contact me or provide assistance in any way. I can't help but think about veteran-ran organizations like Gallant Few, Team RWB, Team Rubicon, Lead the Way Fund, and more, and how much of a positive impact they make with a fraction of a percent of the budget that the VA has. We must begin to rely on ourselves and our fellow war fighters for help the way we did before. The system is broken, it is on us to create a new system ensuring that the values that we sacrificed for do not dissipate into the porous soil of our society the way the blood of our brethren has in lands foreign.

On Assimilation · 214

Acknowledgments

So many people are deserving of thanks in regards to this book being written. A good friend told me that there is no such thing as good writing, just good editing. That being said, Matt Sanders and Marty Skovlund deserve most of the credit for these pages. They both worked tirelessly to ensure that this document flowed correctly. Additionally, thank you Christina Cooke, Brooke Fabra, Charles Faint, and Leonard Benton for providing valuable feedback throughout
the writing process.

Thank you to my good friend Jarred Taylor at Article 15 Clothing for putting together the cover art and providing a frumpy, dejected looking veteran for a model.

Of course, thank you Jameson Irish Whiskey for keeping me company through so many late night writing sessions.

Preview from *First Train out of Denver*

My right knee sinks in the soft sand under the weight of the overly full pack; senses are awakened for the first time in years. The moon provides the perfect amount of illumination for tonight's mission. Covering my sector, scanning from left to right for any possible threats, another Ranger behind me doing the same. The two of us scan the shadows as the scent of something resembling sawdust hangs in the air. The percussion of a pounding heart sends a shock wave throughout my body every half second with the ferocity of the bass drum in a Metallica song. If the police find us, we are done for. This is what being alive feels like. This is a sensation I had almost forgot was possible; the cool night air lifting the sweat from my neck sending a chill down my spine.

It's just passed midnight and we are using an old box car for cover in a train yard as we wait for the right time to board the east bound vessel. The sudden cool breeze is a surprise for a June evening in Denver. The fresh coffee in my travel mug does well to stave off the cold. It is also doing well to sober me up. I knew if I started drinking earlier that I wouldn't be able to turn it off. Handing the mug back to Marty, he gladly takes a sip. At nearly six and a half feet tall Marty is an imposing force, even while on a knee.

"It's time!" Instinctively we pop up from security mode and flip switch into a direct action mentality. Operating under the cover of darkness in hostile environments isn't new for either of us; we know the risk and as well as what's at stake. Marty takes the lead and climbs between two train cars as I stay within an arms distance of his pack. The margin for error here is nonexistent. Neither of us have any experience stowing away on a train, a fact that is easily recognizable if anyone is watching the awkward nature that we climb aboard and attempt to open the door.

"We're in!" Marty exclaims. Breathing heavily, we look around to see if the clamoring that the over packed bags made had alerted anyone to our location. The minutes seem like hours waiting for the train to depart. We begin to let their guard down after nearly half an hour. If anyone had seen us they would have caught us by now. The fatigue of too many late nights is catching up to me now, too many nights searching for comfort at the bottom of a bottle. My eyelids became magnets, drawing toward each other. Just as they connect the door swings open. The backlit outline figure of a man appears from nowhere. Quite calmly he asks, "Can you turn on that light for me?" Marty finds the switch and follows the man's request. He leans over to grab a clipboard hanging from the wall that had gone previously unnoticed in the blackout conditions. The ragged conductor signs a form, places the clipboard back in its place and says, "Have a good night guys," then closes the door behind him.

"Well that was odd." Mary utters in a confused tone. I can't help but think that we are being set up somehow. The discussion begins if we should exit the train. We decide that we should just stay put; if he wanted us off, he would have told us to leave. He didn't even act surprised that we were here. Despite the excitement, it didn't take long before my eyelids met once again. Using an old tan jacket as a pillow, I sprawl out on the floor of the push car and wait for the train to begin moving.

Two hours of hard sleep later, the back door that Marty was propped up against flings open. The all too familiar authoritative voice of a law enforcement officer, shining the brightest flashlight I had ever seen, commands us off the train. Marty piles out of the tiny door awkwardly. I choose to move slowly and deliberately. I know what this looks like and I'm not willing to get shot over this. Collecting the now filthy tan jacket from the dirty floor, I show the officer that I have no weapon, put on my jacket and collect the large red backpack that once again barely fit through the back door of the train.

Sitting on a pile of stones like two overgrown teenagers that are out past curfew, when the lecture from the officer about trespassing begins. I wasn't paying attention, all I could think about was the last time I was arrested for trespassing and how expensive it was.

What am I even doing here? A week ago I had an amazing beach house in Costa Rica, now I'm homeless, unemployed and about to be arrested for train hopping at midnight in Denver, Colorado.

Coming Soon from Blackside Publishing:

From Leo Jenkins:
Tales from the Bottom of the Bottle
First Train out of Denver
Working Title: The Story of a Female EOD Tech
Working Title: An Insider's Perspective of the CIA
During the War on Terror.

From Other Writers:
The Bearded Conservative: Marty Skovlund
Voices from the Shadows: Charlie Faint
Briar Lake (fiction): Cora Kane
Art of War: TBA
Working Title: The Story of a Nirvana Guitarist turned
Special Operator